Garden
DISRUPTORS
THE REBEL MISFITS WHO TURNED SOUTHERN HORTICULTURE ON ITS HEAD

Augustus Jenkins Farmer, III

Cover photo: Marilyn Oliveros of Paisa Photography

Cover models: Kellen Goodell and Samuel Schafer

Cover and interior design: Marc Cardwell

Cover location: the garden of Bo Lauder, Charleston, SC

Copyright 2023 by Augustus Jenkins Farmer III

Independently published: Jenks Farmer Publications

Development and content editing: Kevin Sharpe

Copy editing: Margaret O'Shea and Trish Mclaughlin.

ISBN 979-8-218-30216-0

Dedication

For my family, the one I was born to and the one I chose. You gave me
the foundation to grow and to tell stories about gardens.

Author's Note

Most of this book was written just before or during the isolation of the Covid lockdown. It was a time when we needed connections. Warm reunions happened in cold outdoor gatherings, through technology connections, and long phone calls. Writing this book brought many old friends back into my life. We recalled stories, people, and quirky moments that became part of this story. Almost thirty years after the fact, that time of quiet gave us time to remember. Thank you all.

I've done my best to follow what seem to me to be loose standards of creative non-fiction writing. Most of the people in this book agreed to have their personal stories shared. Some spent hours reading after I'd finally filtered their reminiscings through my words. Thank you for your lasting influence and continued support.

Most of the scenes and people are real. But a few are amalgamations. A few people are described, not named, and a few names are changed. Choosing stories and characters from the dozens of crucial people involved was an arduous challenge that had to be done to tell a good story.

For the sake of storytelling, I've used quotes, most of which are representative of the feelings and intentions of conversations as I recall them.

These sorts of quotes, and amalgamations, along with timeline compression, advance the story in ways necessarily compressed to fit the pages.

To all the gardeners, volunteers, donors, and administrators who made Riverbanks Botanical Garden possible, thank you. I cherish our memories, but more importantly, millions of people from all walks treasure the joy and inspiration they find in the Garden.

❧

Table of Contents

01: Bent Palmetto in the Rain

We say "dog years" when we mean the kind of time that passes quickly. I am a relatively young man, turning 55. In dog years I'm a centenarian.

I've also heard older folks refer to donkey years, reversing the equation. They say, "We've been friends for donkey years," to describe the slow movement of time. I like the idea but prefer to relate it to long lived plants. Magnolias, the most ancient of trees, live for centuries. When I feel a middle age ache, I remind myself that in magnolia years I'm only 32.

Today, 30 years after building the Riverbanks Botanical Garden, if you and I walk through the Garden together, we'd enjoy the new plantings and work of the young staff. But I'm helpless to stop the little movie clips that play in my head. I can't help seeing the raw, red clay; frail baby plants; and compost-covered gardeners of my day. Memories of our ragtag crew come to life in my mind. Sweet, painful, even frightening moments from decades ago. A different world ago. Magnolia years, maybe palmetto years, ago.

Back then, when we were putting it all together, the crew would stand in the nursery, hold two trees near each other, and say, "Do you like how these look together?"

I might reply, "Sharp. But how's it going to look in five years when that princess tree crowds and stunts the cherry?"

Five years seemed so, so far away.

Every new guy who joined the crew would say, "The palmetto trunks look just like big dicks sticking up." Only the crudest redneck frat boy or recently released convict would say out loud, "Dang, look at that curved one. I hope mine never looks like that."

Reasonable me would respond, "Shut up y'all. In five years, they won't look like dicks at all. They'll be stately gentlemen. Their leaves will make that crinkly sound, like old men rubbing their beards. Every bride will want their photo taken here."

Today one of those palmettos curves near the ground and bends out over the pool. It defies gravity. Its leaves, like a full head of hair, ought to make it slowly tip into the fountain. I can't comprehend the force that created this arc, but I have loved it from the moment I saw it and knew it belonged in the Garden.

Young palmettos grow slowly in their first years. The black pearl seed germinates, but unlike other plants, it starts to grow down. It's a root-like thing, bone white, and it continues to grow down, then further down. When it finds the right spot, it makes another pearl. This one is white, and it has to start all over again. It grows new roots. Finally, six months or a year later, a single leaf starts growing up. Then from above ground, we get to see some green that looks like nothing more than hard grass. At this point it still mostly grows below ground, girth up, making a trunk. That trunk might thicken for five years before it starts growing up. Then it grows an inch a year.

But this little gravity-defying guy hit something when he finally started growing up. A barrier he had no control over. On the banks of a swampy South Carolina lagoon, that might have been the bone of a giant gator or a thick magnolia root. Something tried to stop him, so he grew crooked. Eighty or a hundred years later, I saw him in a palm tree nursery, loved his curve, and tagged him along with a dozen other palm trees to be delivered to the garden.

When I walk through the garden today, I see what you see. A stately palm with intriguing curvature defying gravity over a splashing fountain and pool. In my head, though, I hear Tommy's Lowcountry brogue as I recall the day we planted this palm. Tommy was a retired prison guard and hostage negotiator. Gray in the temples, he still carried a country boy swagger and oozed confidence.

When I talked to him I would slip back into the slurred accent and cadence I'd worked to erase. "Tommy, how we gonna get this three-ton, lop-sided, palmetto log over that brand new wall that Jim imported from England, then lower it ten feet; set it just so, safe and secure; straighten it up; and hold it in place while these jokers build a wooden support?"

Tommy either knew the answer, or he'd figured it out. He leaned over the wall, looking down at the crew and me. "Boys, stand back. I don't wanna have to pull y'all out from under anything. This monster wouldn't leave much of you for me to pull."

————

Three more skinny, young guys in cargo pants and big boots scaled down the wall to help. Our boots got heavier as wet clay caked on them. Melodie and Jim, standing above, let down shovels, drills, and wooden posts for leverage and support. We looked up into a cloudy sky, mud-heavy boots holding us in place, as Tommy drove a teetering backhoe to the wall with a two-ton palmetto hanging horizontally from the big black bucket. The backhoe groaned and started to tip forward. The tree made the backhoe front-heavy. Tommy knew what to do and called out, "We need some fellas with meat on their bones up here."

A couple of our heavier folks climbed up on the seat, hugging Tommy. They were counterweights. Tommy swung two tons of palmetto over our heads like a wrecking ball in a political cartoon. One of the taller guys extended a two-by-four and steadied the palmetto. Now that it seemed stable, Tommy throttled down. That's when we heard the screeching. We looked up, past the swinging tree to a swarm of ten thousand black grackles screeching as they dropped out of the sky to roost in our woods.

Then something really bad came from above. Rain.

In sync, we all yelled, "Fuck. This is a horror movie."

Melodie, my college friend, my confidant and peer, standing on the back of the tractor, hugging Tommy, could always lighten a mood with a funny quip. "Do I feel rain or is that crow pee?"

Then she called out to me, "Do we keep going?"

I yelled to everyone, "Keep planting y'all! What else can we do? Leave this palmetto dangling to crush the balustrades and the pool and the fountain edge? Nobody's gonna melt in the rain."

All of us guys down in the hole took off our shirts. Better to be skin slick than have a wet and muddy t-shirt clinging tightly, constricting movement. We planted.

————

Today, 30 years later, I'm probably about the age Tommy was when we planted this garden together. Today I walk by the ginkgo grove and envision Tommy locking us all inside an office near the newly planted trees as camo-clad troopers storm by in search of an escaped convict. Today I see those palmettos, ginkgos, and magnolias towering stately and reaching the prime of their lives. Tommy is gone. Cancer got him about ten years ago.

Back then, young trees and shrubs were lean and lanky. Plants have awkward teenage years, too. I think of touring the society ladies, the donors, who'd walk by our grungy crew and exclaimed, "How beautiful! Y'all are so smart to know how to make this garden!"

I know now they were telling white lies, though maybe a few were actually able to see beyond the leafless palmetto dicks and scraggly young plants. Some of them, like us, like any real gardener, could envision the garden magnolia years into the future.

Today the plantings have filled out, trees cast shade, and shrubs overflow their spaces. Lots of things I loved have matured and died. I'm filled out now, too, as are likely the society ladies, though most of them are gone.

Back then, in 1992, I was a young, idealistic queer man who had run away from his conservative roots in the Deep South, then returned home to South Carolina for a unique opportunity — to build a botanical garden on the banks of a spectacular river.

In the '90s, gardens were being built all over the South, but this project was different. Columbia, South Carolina, was a small, provincial town with a sort of 1950s flair. Stores didn't open on Sundays until after church. Interracial marriage had been legalized for only five years by state law. From my perspective, every adult woman seemed to be a Baptist Sunday school teacher and every man had a gun rack in his rear window and a chew circle in his back pocket.

My plan was to stay less than two years, 18 months at most, to live quietly, make a garden, and avoid the conservatives, rednecks, military guys, church wives, golfers, and even A-list gays like my antique-dealing uncles. I didn't want to be like any of these folks or to grow around their barriers.

As it turned out, there were a few of the city leaders, including the Zoo director Satch Krantz, who wanted things to be different. I didn't get it then, but that this small town hired two gay guys to define, build, and be the public face of the city's new botanical garden spoke volumes.

As Riverbanks Botanical Garden's first Curator of Horticulture, I got to hire a crew of creative misfits. On an isolated site in the woods, by a river, near the ruins of a Confederate uniform factory, under Spanish moss, we bonded. We realized that we had the power to redefine garden styles and aesthetics, which, in this place and at that time, were remnants of the last century: Formality and dominion over nature defined beauty.

Walls of azaleas got all the love. Garden club ladies and Camellia Society gentlemen had set the standards. Vestiges of Jim Crow, racism, and elitism defined gardens. Believe it or not, even certain plants in the South sometimes had racist and classist stigmas.

Our band of garden disruptors challenged all that with flowers. We found support from unexpected people who jumped in as volunteers. The garden grew. We grew.

Now, magnolia years later, as I walk through this garden, I am excited by what the new young horticulturists plant. I see their visions. I see a newly planted scrawny magnolia tree, a species hybrid that didn't even exist back in the day — a magnolia with pink flowers that smell like banana pudding. What sort of young mind even dreamed that up, much less created this new vision? I won't be around long enough to see it grow grandly. But I'm around now to tell the stories of a team of misfits who found solace and a sense of purpose in planting this garden magnolia years ago.

02: Escaping the South

I grew up surrounded by the beauty of a farm in the deep South. But I also grew up seeing around me that the South is a place that, in many ways, is wounded. It's suffering. In pain. Like a stately old water oak, it can look strong and graceful, but the outer bark is nothing more than veneer wrapping a cavern where rattlesnakes, roaches, and oozing black fungus wait, ready to strike, catapult, or quietly eject infectious spores. So when I finally got away from rural South Carolina, I told myself I would never come back. Maybe for Christmas and funerals, but certainly not for good.

At Cub Scout camp this little gay boy could fit in. Junior high soccer? Yeah, I could play, but I never felt part of the team. When a tenth-grade Baptist school teacher stood me up in front of the class and said with a smirk, "Based on what you've told me, your family cannot be Christians," I started the countdown to escape. Even the old farmer I worked for — the one I bonded with over calving, hay baling, and scuppernong picking — shook his head in disdain when he saw that my 17-year-old ear was freshly pierced. I bided my time among the hayseeds another three or four years, then found my way out of the pain endemic in this place of intolerance and swamp gas.

What is swamp gas? Literally, it is methane gas from centuries of slowly rotting leaves under black muck in a magnolia swamp. It bubbles up like spittle from tiny tunnels in the mud. Sometimes the gas glows at night. Country people around where I grew up tell tales to explain the glow. They say it's a dead railroad man swinging his lantern, searching for a lost love. Or some tell of tiny fairies floating in orbs. I knew better, and I would never miss an opportunity to explain the science of swamp gas to help these people rise above ghost stories and fairy tales. They didn't listen.

As a boy, I had a few people in my life who helped me see a better world. My Momma made me go away at 18. She said, "You just have to. You'll find a place." She knew I'd fit in somewhere, with people like me. Before that though, I had found people like me in books. I dream-lived Maupin's Tales of the City, in his open, loving community on Barbary Lane. There's a quote in that book about finding the family you want instead of sticking with the family you were dealt. I wanted accepting, adventure-seeking, fun people for my found family.

Once I discovered some freedom in college I tried Atlanta, Hilton Head, Columbia, even D.C., which for young Southerners is like a northern city, but still close enough to home in climate and geography so as not to be too scary. I even did the requisite vagabonding through Africa and Europe. But for work and for graduate school, I thought the South was best for me.

Raleigh, North Carolina, seemed like a fantastic landing spot since it was the home of my mentor, the renowned horticulturist Dr. J.C. Raulston, But J.C. said, "No, you cannot go to grad school under me. Raleigh isn't far enough. Go to Seattle. It's the center of the garden world right now. It's full of creative, openly gay people. You'll fall in love. If you ever come back, you'll be a teacher, a leader. You'll bring the change you so need to see."

That wasn't the answer I wanted, so I kept looking for an exciting and cool place.

Weeks later in rural Georgia, Callaway Gardens held a conference that drew professional horticulturists from across the United States. I attended on a day ticket. A random seating on a tour bus put me beside a balding man who introduced himself as Dr. Harold Tuckey. He asked to hear my story. He listened to my dreams. Then he said, "I've started a new horticulture program in Seattle. If your grades are good enough, I could probably get you financial aid. Come and do graduate school there."

We might have talked further, but suddenly, out of nowhere, a slow train hit our bus and spun us around. We were shaken up and whisked off in different vehicles. Of everything that happened on this crazy day, the thing that most stuck with me was the old professor's offer.

Now I may not believe in headless railroad men eternally swinging lanterns through the swamp, but I know there's always more out there than meets the eye. And I know that sometimes it's better just to listen and trust the signs. When two smart men, who lived on opposite sides of the country, said the same thing, and a train seared it into my memory, I figured I ought to pay attention. On top of that, at the same conference I met a handsome, curly-haired graduate student from Seattle. There were just too many signs. So I enrolled in graduate school, got a map, and started figuring out how to get a loan and move to Seattle.

———

A year later, I was on my way. In my VW's rear view mirror swirled Kentucky green, Nebraska straw, and clouds of Rocky Mountain dirt-road dust. Then at dawn one morning I saw the liberated me in that rear view mirror. Destiny sparkled as I crested the dry Cascades and dove into the soft gray mists of the super-cool and magical Emerald City.

Seattle fit me. I fit Seattle. They had the coolest, efficient city buses so I could go anywhere for free. Better yet, I could talk to any stranger, except the crazy ones, and they'd most likely be educated and liberal. Just that was a stunning contrast between life back home. Book stores, wheatgrass bars, out gay men who acted like men, and the Center for Urban Horticulture (part of the University of Washington) were all part of my own little paradise. It was liberation.

Jovial Dr. John A. Wott would become my graduate advisor and friend. He walked me through elegant, Chinese-inspired pavilions and under groves of vine maples. This tree and its form were new to me — beauties that reached straight up then bent, splayed, and made lacy, canopy-like vines on an invisible pergola. Dr. Wott showed me the second largest horticulture library on the West Coast, right above my communal graduate student office. He gave me the royal tour and said, "Part of your job will be hosting and touring visiting professionals. You'll be leading campus and off-site tours. We have a group who wants to see the Skagit Valley tulip fields and the Chinese Garden in Vancouver. Get out there. Explore. It's part of your job."

Did I say I was in heaven?

I was representing John and the Center, cold calling horticulture stars like Dan Hinkley and Bellevue Botanic's creative team of Charles Price and Glenn Withey. I got to pick up English provocateur Christopher Lloyd at the airport. I got along great with all these heavy hitters. Maybe it had a little to do with my accent, which until that point, I didn't know I even had. Every single person who heard me speak seemed fascinated by it.

Elizabeth Miller, patron of the garden arts, introduced me to her proteges, two of whom I'd later date. When Apple released their first laptop, this doyeenne of northwestern gardens bought one for me. This truly was the Emerald City.

A fascinating and intentionally created wetland separated the Center for Urban Horticulture from the larger university campus. At its edge, on Lake Washington, were floating sphagnum islands. I could jump on them and make the ground jiggle like jello. The shore consisted of engineered layers of dirt topped with native plants. It all capped an old landfill. One morning, John said, "Jenks, after the garden tours, would you take Dr. Raven across the wetland to the medicinal plant garden?"

"Are you kidding me?" I thought, "Dr. Peter Raven?" My job was to walk with the most esteemed plantsmen in the world. Even my "new" used REI rain jacket, in all its crinkliness, stood straighter.

Dr. Raven and I set out across the marsh. There was no wind on Lake Washington that day. No mist either. Halfway through the maze, I stopped, bent down, and took out my lighter. "See the little bubbles in the mud? Watch this?" I flicked the lighter, and the bubbles hissed and caught fire. "This wetland was created on top of an old Seattle dump." I said, "You can light the bubbles on fire because the organic decomposition makes methane gas."

"Not exactly." He corrected gently. "It's life. The methane comes not from the trash, but from bacteria that digest the refuse of long-gone suburbanites. Life is life."

Oh yeah, I thought to myself, I knew that. Swamp gas.

On campus and around town, amazing plants spilled out of every crook and cranny. In addition to exploring moss gardens on islands, I attended Japanese moon-watching parties, and discovered city community gardens overflowing with crazy vegetables. I had found the open, creative, uninhibited, sparkling people who seemed to have all come here for the same reason — to find themselves. Having come to find out, some of them wanted to find me, too.

03: Falling in Love in Seattle

My van was first in line on the dock to drive on board, so I parked facing the expanse of Puget Sound. Seattle sparkled like Oz in the crystal clear summer light. Beside me, in the bike lane, some guy on a big motorcycle leaned over and let a tiny dog out of his jacket. I loved watching strangers here and learning that Seattle-ites and their dogs take travel over crashing waves for granted. Most folks left their vehicles and went to the enclosed upper-deck coffee shop. This was adventure to me, so I stayed outside to soak it all in and squatted by the rail to talk to the dog, feeling the salty breeze against my face.

I'd led this garden tour of 24 horticulturists all day and had definitely noticed this one man in particular. Kevin. He was in his mid-30s. I even talked to him. A small guy in a denim jacket, big brogan boots, and a thick Scandinavian blond beard. He really knew his plants but unlike everyone else, he wasn't showing it off. His eyes sparkled. He had a shy smile, and he paid attention when I talked. Was he showing extra interest in me? Or maybe, like everyone else, he was just smiling at my accent.

"Did you already know Hinkley through the Center?" he asked. This was the most personal thing he'd said all day. No wedding ring. Then he steered the conversation back to plants. Damn it. No sign of anything but professional interest. He did lean in extra close to talk into my ear. But with the wind and sea gulls, that simply could have been practical. More plant talk. But a handsome man and plant talk? I disembarked the ferry half an hour later still with a hard on.

Back at work I pointed his name out on the registration list to Dr. Wott and said, "I don't even know if he's gay. I don't want to do anything unprofessional. Maybe he'll sign up for another tour, and we'll see how it goes."

Dr. Wott knew most of the professionals who signed up for classes and tours, but he didn't know Kevin. He smiled, "I think you're being very Southern about this. There's his phone number. Use it. If he doesn't want to go on a date, he'll say so."

I never called because Kevin, whom I'd hardly seen around before, signed up for several classes and tours that I'd set up. We found out soon enough that we were made for each other. Things happened fast. Garden tour dates turned into weekends of naked camping on Mt. Baker, nights at art festivals, and Carl Smool Day of the Dead parades. Besides being as handsome as a Viking, Kevin inspired the unexplored artist in me. He painted and sculpted. I loved being in his studio. He had a truck filled with tools. He was drawn to physical work like bricklaying and gardening. I knew that his sculptures required carpentry and furniture skills because my Daddy made furniture. Kevin had the skills and competence that I admired in Dad and other farm men I'd known. But Kevin used his skills with a beautiful, positive, masculine energy that connected him to Mother Earth.

I moved in and we settled into an art-filled life with three kittens and his funky garden. I took the bus to work. He gardened and made art. We lived in the Central District, a poor area that was the only place Seattle's very few Black people congregated. It was the only place I could find catfish, cornbread mix, and frozen fried okra at the grocery. Kevin refused to eat any of it and teased me about saying mash when he thought the proper word was push. I loved that he saw quirks that I didn't know I had. We were vegetarians, of course, and so skinny that we could cuddle and sleep together in a single bed.

We had a romantic, beautiful year. But deep down, I knew what was on the horizon.

———

I'd come here to escape to a wonderful world, but I'd also come to develop my dream career. Through my job at the Center, I'd built national connections. I had a thesis up for publication in an international botanical garden journal and a head full of cool new ideas that lots of gardens or any kind of living museum would value.

I didn't want to see graduate work and my soon-to-be master's degree as a crisis. I was poised to start a career in a major botanical garden. How could that be a crisis?

The recession years of the early '90s made it tough to get a job in Seattle.

I looked at public gardens from Vancouver to northern California. We didn't really talk about it a lot, but we both knew I was probably going to have to leave. Kevin, like me, had run from a repressive world. He'd defined himself and found his friends, garden clients, and art patrons. He was settled and comfortable. Though he said he'd consider moving to northern California, we both loved Seattle. I tried to be creative in the job search.

On one crazy day I drove a few hours north to interview for a job at Rainy Pass. My little VW climbed to 5,500 feet and stopped at a welcome center and overlook. That day, it was empty, but in summer endless road trippers stopped to eat lingonberry ice cream and view extensive gardens. The interviewer pointed to a bent-over Douglas fir and said, "It got ruined by a rock slide last winter. You realize everything here, every single thing, is under feet of snow from December till March?"

Leaving that interview, driving down the snowy mountain, my heart sank. I didn't think or say it, but I knew what I was about to do. I needed to quit fooling myself. I had to admit that I was the ass who was going to choose career over love.

Back in the grad student office, I picked up a new issue of a national public garden newsletter. There in the black and white of one paragraph was the job with my name on it — a brand new botanical garden seeking to hire an entire staff. The new curator would have lots of creative input. This would be a chance to do research and build core plant collections while exploring new plants. I exceeded the requirements. When I saw the location, I knew the competition would be slim. After all, what sort of urbane, educated, up-and-coming, young curator in their right mind would want to move, or, in my case, to move backwards to South Carolina?

My old college friend, Jim Martin, was in charge of getting the new botanical garden off the ground. I called him immediately, and he filled me in: "We've been working on this since you left, Jenks. Now, the funding is set, the land secured. We have seven million dollars and 70 acres. It'll be unlike anything in South Carolina–the first one to be built since the '50s. Apply. You can be a part of the vision."

"Why didn't you call me to let me know?" I asked.

Jim was frank: "You left here saying you'd never come back. Besides, you're thriving out there, and you always hated the South."

But he knew how to reel me in. "You always complained about all the boring green boxwood gardens here," he said. "Do you want to help change that?" Then he added, "The South has changed. It isn't so bad now."

I'd always been the radical with earrings and eyeliner. I had always been the one trying to lead head-in-the-sand Southerners on a path most of them didn't want to take, and I had always failed. Now, at least in a garden sense, I might be able to show all those backwoods farmers, boring azalea lovers, camellia queens, and old fogies the beauty that horticulture could be. I could be the worldly visionary they needed.

Kevin said he would try to make it work. With the gentle Seattle rain dulling the morning light, I turned to him and said, as if to bolster both of our spirits, "When it's winter here, you could stay in the sunny South for a month or so."

"I have cats," he paused, adding the punctuation of silence. "We have cats. And we have a bathroom full of orchids."

I knew he wasn't on board. I sensed that he was feeling abandoned. I was desperate for this to work out for us. "Actually, August is rough in South Carolina, so I could spend that here," I said.

The feelings hung in the air and lingered for days. Eventually, they started to settle, shifting into conversation, less raw and more constructive, about trying to make the job and our separation work. Seattle friends joined in. And despite their lack of support and their seemingly endless, creative, ways of saying that I was crazy for taking a job back in the Deep South, Kevin and I developed a plan. I would go for the construction phase,

24 months tops. We'd write, send drawings, talk on the phone, and travel to each other four times a year. All of our friends, with the exception of one, still thought I was crazy.

That one was a born-and-bred New Orleans queen, 15 years my senior, and he jumped on board with my plan. He had ideas of his own and wanted to turn my solo drive to South Carolina into an accompanied cross-country extravaganza filled with class and style: a fabulous road trip through America's low-brow roadside attractions:

"The drama of it all, Jenks. The drama!"

04: Emotional Road Trip Back South

My friend Robert was an erudite, cultured, classically sarcastic gentleman. He was a collector of textiles and haute couture. He was the recently retired director of the Decorative Arts Museum and had escaped to Seattle from New Orleans decades ago. He had made a fabulous life. He was the kind of guy who owned champagne sets, a silver spoon warmer, and an acerbic wit.

Anytime I visited, thoughtful Robert served snacks in a sweetgrass basket, knowing its Geechee craftwork reminded me of home. Robert was an up-to-date, self-aware version of Daddy's brother, my somewhat pretentious gay uncle, and his antique dealing lover. Robert melded the pretenses of the old queens I'd known with a self-awareness expertly conveyed with a wink of the eye at the absurdity of all of his fancy trappings.

Like so many of those older queens, whom I now realize had been lifelong mentors, he had AIDS. It was a death sentence, but Robert stayed healthy for a long time. He took care of himself and sold his cat. Back then we knew so little about the disease that we thought you couldn't have a cat if you had AIDS for fear of contracting toxoplasmosis.

Robert launched into planning the ultimate American road trip. It was obvious that he was ready to leave. What was not obvious was why he would leave such an open and understanding place. Here, in Seattle, I'd been a part of support groups, the Chicken Soup Brigade, and I'd felt the love people here would lavish on the dying. Public leaders in the South still didn't even whisper the name AIDS, and judgmental Southern families laid blame and shame.

But Robert seemed thrilled by the prospect of this buddy trip. On the folded-down back seat of my VW Fox, Robert had set up a little travel planning office complete with a bar. As he put a few cubes of ice in a glass, he said, "We are not paying for ice. I read that we can raid motels for ice." His maps and AAA TripTiks™ spilled from his Christian Louboutin™ porte-document case. Robert had never done anything tacky in his life. ("Well, nothing I can recall at this moment." he'd say, with a long, slow, sideways glance and a finger on his lips.) Tacky just wasn't his style. So this roadside-attraction-studded road trip would be a first for him.

On our first stop, just over the Cascades, we wandered around Dick and Jane's Spot among towering walls of bedazzled bicycle wheels spinning in the arid winds. Days later we ate roasted corn at The Corn Palace and then turned south to catch the motor courts on Route 66. It would be a zig-zaggy route but this was Robert's Grand Tour of the roadside attractions of America. Both his first taste of slumming and his slum finale.

———

On the Fourth of July a long day of driving left us tired, but we couldn't pass Yellowstone without a glimpse. We illegally parked on a remote northern overlook, and Robert made us martinis in a silver shaker. Sunset painted itself in purples and golds. "It's a Remington painting," Robert said as he pointed to the food basket. "Pass the pimento cheese." We said goodbye to our West with a toast as it started to snow. This snow in July, a wonder for Southerners like us, subdued any sadness.

A day later, we pulled over and stood waist-deep on a plain of waving grain. Looking out into the powerful infinity and the majesty of this country, we cried like babies. "For the purple mountains' majesty," we told ourselves, for the bounty, and the spacious sky. We ignored our own loss.

I dropped Robert off with an art collector friend in New Orleans. As I drove away under the bent live oaks of Louisiana, I pulled over onto a narrow highway shoulder with a ditch of black-tipped Bahia grass and a few tall carnivorous pitcher plants poking through. I wanted to get out and look but I was afraid of snakes and alligators.

Robert's map was on the floor. It was ticked with all the sites and places that had made up this trip. No more exciting stops now. I was on the red line headed home alone. And I'd just left my friend Robert to die. I cried into my steering wheel, this time not ignoring the truth. I cried for the loss to come, for being alone, for making bad decisions, for the knowledge that I'd chosen the hard road. If I'd ever had a hope chest, it would now be in a dumpster behind a motel on Route 66.

Nothing new in the rear view mirror now as I continued on. Just two-lane roads and too-familiar, one-light towns with three First Baptist churches and, on the edge of town, a Little Pigs Barbecue Hut surrounded by four-wheel-drive pickups. Further out I would always see a gravel lot and a concrete block building, maybe with the words "Soundtrack Supper Club" painted on one side. The name and isolation would tell me that each one of those buildings was a bar for Black people.

In a Mississippi gas station two old men stood at the counter talking about the headlines in a gossip rag newspaper. The White man with suspenders holding up his Wranglers leaned toward the old Black cashier. They greeted me as I walked in, then went back to their conversation about the fuss over Magic Johnson's AIDS revelation.

One of the men said, "Musta' been some horseplay in the locker room. Fellas do that, you know." "Umhum. But he should'a known better," the other responded. "Ya' play, ya' pay."

"Sho 'nough." They seemed to agree that AIDS was Magic Johnson's fault, that he deserved its death sentence, and he should just suffer.

I put my Coke on the floor and walked out. What had I done leaving Seattle? I had found what I was longing for and left it. They were right. Not these old coots, but my older gay friends back in Seattle. I would never change anyone or anything here. I should turn around, make another fun road trip with Robert, and admit I was going backward by coming back to the South. This was the time to drive back to Seattle.

At that moment, the hurt came back. It hadn't come only from strangers like that old Black man at the counter. He could have been one of my parents' friends. It hadn't come only from the White guy. He could have been my father. What hurt was being familiar with these kinds of people and knowing they would have just as easily shamed and blamed me. These were strangers. But the same kind of hurt came from my mother, sisters, cousins, friends, mentors, and teachers in South Carolina. Most would never put it into words. Most loved me and would welcome me back. But I felt that their love came with strings:

"We love you. But."

"Toughen up, boy. Play baseball."

"Find a nice girl. Get married."

"Bite your tongue."

On the monkey bars in fifth grade Ann-Cecilia Carrol said what she meant. She told me, "I like ye but I think ye'r a faggot."

Two words in her sentence confused me. First, the word ye. Anne-Cecilia lived in a Southern oddity, a village of gypsies called Irish Travelers, hidden in the Deep South. They all spoke an Irish Gaelic, redneck, pidgin brogue. Faggot was also new to me. Someone explained the word. It hurt and I came back strong trying to hurt her, "But people call you names, too: gypsies, trashy cons. And you're gonna be married off to a grown man when you're in sixth grade!. Why would you want to call me names? To hurt me like I know you've been hurt, Anne-Cecilia?"

While it was true that some of these people seemed happy that I was coming back, the rub, the hurt, for me was that they wanted only parts of me, like my gardening skills. They didn't want me, all of me.

———

My Seattle friends tried to warn me about this. Most knew the South only through headlines, or through my years of complaints and horror stories. Despite my past experience growing up in the South, I couldn't accept their arguments and defended my decision when they said:

"It's going to be the same, Jenks. You cannot change it. "

"You'll get beat up."

"You'll have to live in the closet."

"Look what they're doing to Shannon Faulkner. Why should she have to fight to get admitted to the Citadel? It's a public college, for God's sake! A public college that fights in court to keep women out."

"Do you really think you can change things?"

"That's a long, long way to try to keep a relationship going."

I'd had role models for leaving and living as a Southern expat in the Northwest. But there were no role models for going back. André Leon Talley, Truman Capote, were all famous escapees. Armistead Maupin didn't live in his birthplace of North Carolina but in California. His lauded debut of the Tales in the City mini-series was banned from South Carolina ETV, and an Alabama station called it a "slick piece of homosexual propaganda."

Why couldn't I simply accept that there is a reason that Southerners like me don't go back home?

John Fairey, one of my mentors and the renowned founder of Peckerwood Gardens, told me, "I have never been and will never go home to South Carolina. No. Not even to visit a garden that you make."

All those men who never came home had a much deeper hurt than I did. And the older men who actually never left the South, like my uncles, stayed and nursed the pain. Both groups had done things to make my life easier. They'd done things at home and from afar that helped change the South and gave me, even if I wasn't thrilled about it, the possibility of going home again.

I knew I needed them now. So I put them in a little support group in my head. Not only the real uncles but Talley, Quentin Crisp, and Paul Lynde. They became The Uncles, a chorus, a rock band, an all-star group of advisors offering protection and advice — hard-won wisdom based on what they had done when they were alive.

The Uncles had mastered catty commentary because it amused them. In their phrases and the tones in which they spoke them, The Uncles had the power to express more than the meaning of the words. Perhaps just as empowering, they expected others to get it. If you didn't get it, you didn't count.

It was time for me to call on The Uncles to help me through the gauntlet of self-satisfied old White men, sanctimonious Sunday school teachers, vapid good ol' boys, and huntin'-for-a-husband Southern party girls. They all scared me, and I had a sinking feeling in the pit of my stomach that I was headed back to a place I was not supposed to be. I hoped that feeling was wrong.

05: First Day Working Backstage at the Zoo

It was late summer when I drove down a bland exit ramp onto a desolate frontage road, across a bumpy railroad track, and into Riverbanks Zoo's main parking lot, where even the public ticket booth seemed forlorn. Inside the gates, though, magic happened. Bamboo groves shaded tigers, flamingos nested in a palm oasis, and a curving tunnel covered with blooming wisteria draped over visitors each spring.

My employee entry consisted of gauntlets of double fences and, without a badge yet, it meant introducing myself to an ex-military security guard, who I could just tell took my shaggy hair as a personal affront. Then there was a requisite pass through a daunting breakroom. Opening that door was like stepping into a high school locker room. Everyone looked up, and no one was impressed. No one seemed happy about the new guy.

Behind the scenes at the Zoo was a wild, self-contained little world. I would soon find out it was a bit like Peyton Place, full of odd creatures. It was an odd collection of loners and misfits. They're the types of people who are often attracted to animal care, finding solace in a rough-and-tumble world through comforting and caring for other misunderstood, lost beings.

The curator of fish told me on the first day in the break room that this botanical garden was the worst mistake the Zoo had ever made. I knew many others in the group we'd come to call the Animal People who felt that way, too. The money and energy going into plants could have been used to upgrade the penguin exhibit or build what the Animal People saw as the holy grail, a gorilla habitat.

I just had to bide my time at the Zoo. I'd move later into my own construction trailer, isolated and safe across the wild and rocky Saluda River. That trailer wouldn't even have a phone. It would just be me and 15 or so new gardeners that I'd get to choose and hire. That was the better part of a magnolia year away.

"We're all sharing an office that is hidden from the Zoo's staff," Jim Martin, the boss, said as he ushered me into the dark auditorium. He pushed open big swinging entry doors. We walked through, then stopped as the doors swung closed behind us, leaving us in darkness, surrounded by the smell of cold carpet. We now saw light under two previously hidden closet doors. One hid a narrow stairway to the auditorium's control room. The other closet held brooms, a stack of plastic chairs, cardboard boxes, and a tight spiral staircase, which ascended to our office. Hamsters and other small mammals would have loved the entry to our office. Apparently, the Small-Mammal People didn't know about this.

"You realize the irony don't you?" I said.

"We are in the closet," he said.

Jim rolled his eyes. "Welcome back, missy," he said.

I knew this was Jim playing a role. Too young to be part of a gay generation who could quote or impersonate Bette Davis, he could still easily slip into queen mode every once in a while. He didn't look the part. Handsome, dirty blond, with thickly haired legs and arms. He was usually in cargo shorts with sharpened Felco pruners and a bulky staff radio strapped on his waist. In truth he looked more like a 30-year-old Crocodile Dundee.

This was the man who'd charmed Columbia into gardening. On the early morning TV show with Susan Audé Fisher or the kid's show with Mr. Knozit, Jim would wow them with freaky plants that ate bugs and trees that grew sausages. The military crowd, the retired crowd, and whoever else watched television at six in the morning loved Jim Martin. He had hidden his sexuality well but at great personal cost. The public loved that he seemed grounded to the earth, but full of possibilities and dreams for Columbia.

We climbed the stairs and sat in the office for a while, talking about how old school the Columbia garden scene remained, and how we would reform it. From this little attic office, from this zoo, Jim had charmed Columbia.

Jim wasn't Columbia's first celebrated gardener by any means. There had been others, back in the 1950s and even earlier. Columbia had a rich history in horticulture. In the 1800s the South Carolina Lunatic Asylum, often known only by its location, Bull Street, operated one of America's first horticultural therapy programs. It was headed by a man who became a local celebrity gardener, the exotic and beloved Oqui Adair.

The Civil War had left farms barren, so when Oqui successfully grew veggies to feed the inmates/patients, he saved the government money and embarrassment. Soon enough, high-powered senators were asking Oqui — rumored to be the only Chinese citizen of the state — to come over and tell them what to plant in their yards, yet were still too wary to invite him inside their homes.

———

Outwardly butch, Jim could cross social barriers. He knew how to slip into different circles as easily as he changed from dirty boots at work to safari outfits for TV. He knew how to act and look the part. He would put on a tailored suit to charm the blueblood garden club ladies, the country club set, and their powerful husbands. He'd do Toastmasters, Rotary, and the Better Business Bureau breakfast group. Afterward they'd send big donations to the garden project, addressed to Jim. These power broker types made things happen, and Jim knew he needed them.

But more importantly, the Zoo and the Garden got support through popular vote. Most people who voted in Richland and Lexington counties — rich, poor, firmly middle — had voted to support a municipal bond that would temporarily raise their taxes to build a botanical garden. Like the Zoo and the city of Columbia, Riverbanks Botanical Garden was to be immensely accessible. Unlike many grandiose gardens of the past, this garden would be a plant haven for soldiers and mechanics, mill workers and teachers, people of all races and ages.

Jim had pushed the idea of the project, painting pictures with broad brushstrokes. He described to donors and politicians an English garden-like paradise complete with a visitor center, fountains, a café, and butterflies — an ideal place for classic and modern candle-lit weddings and parties.

He and the Zoo's director spent years building support. They understood there would be depth to the Garden, a mission, as there had always been with the Zoo's animal collections. In the Zoo, conservation such as captive breeding and reintroduction was a requisite part of daily life. Research delved into mating and environmental interactions. Education programs, classes, and even morning TV shows were focused on raising conservation awareness. Exhibition, which most visitors enjoy, was and is only a part of the picture. Preservation projects in nearby woods and even around the world keep animals' home habitats and ecosystems intact. To remember all the aspects of a living museum like a zoo or botanical garden, it's handy to remember the acronym CREEP — conservation, research, education, exhibition, preservation.

My new job was to be multifaceted. First, I would define the museum functions, including searching for a collection plant group. Second, my new team and I would mix the soils, plant the plants, and cultivate the vision and seeds to create a place for visitors to be immersed in natural beauty.

But at the beginning my work was hashing out the strategy for CREEP. It would be my job to sit in the office and come up with plant groups, families, and themes; drill Jim and Melodie; and pound out a plant mission.

Jim and Melodie (my former college friend and now colleague) had already set some standards. The Zoo's standards were management, insect and animal friendliness, and climate appropriateness. So we followed them in the Garden, too.

The attic office sprawled in a triangle shape. In the deepest recess was a huge drawing table, layered with blueprints and colored pencils. Jim's desk sat in front, complete with a tan phone the size of today's laptops, and very old school, with 30 buttons blinking red.

At the wider end of the office stood Melodie's desk, my desk, and a side table with a coffee pot, boom box, and stacks of Mel's Eric Clapton CDs. This is where I set up an Apple and a time-tested database. That system, shared from J.C. Raulston Arboretum at North Carolina State, managed plant accessions, recordkeeping, and labeling. I set to work reconciling the empty database with plants on the ground, a year's worth of things bought, rooted, seeded, collected in the wild, or accepted from conservation rescue programs and now already growing at the Zoo.

Huddled masses of plants sat crammed behind the scenes in a shady old greenhouse and nursery. Actually, this place made a mockery of the word nursery. Plants held their breath here. Spanish moss shaded the greenhouse roof, and hickory nuts crashed through its glass in autumn. Fading tags and paper records threatened to turn years of detailed plant collecting into a worthless, mongrel shrub mass. That area would be a big challenge to overcome.

My new title was Curator of Botanical Gardens. Organizing someone else's exciting mess is fun for a curator. I have a librarian's love for organization. Getting the chance to form long-term goals and to lay out a strategy for collections made for heady stuff for a curator. And a rare opportunity for a guy who'd just turned 27.

Most of my work was in the hidden office. But I got to explore other hidden places, too.

A zoo is a stage, complete with props and scenery and actors. For example, visitors couldn't tell that Tiger Bamboo Jungle was just a low concrete block building with gunite rocks in front of it. Behind it, though, asphalt paths made it easy for the commissary crew to deliver meals of hay bales, slabs of meat, trays of mice, and extra pumpkins after Halloween. The paths also provided access for the manure crew.

Jim and Melodie introduced me to folks as we walked around on my orientation tour. Among the backstage folks we came upon were Reptile People. They reeked of a musky, swamp odor. "It's the cottonmouths," they said. "Whenever we have to isolate them for exhibit work, they expel this stench through their anal glands. It's a warning we wear all day. You can't wash it out."

———

My guides led me through a spectacular grove of Chinese wingnut trees. Horizontal, gray, muscled branches made a low, flat canopy. Ten-inch strings of jade seed pods dangled just overhead. This was the public side, where trees shaded picnic tables by the thatched roof Safari Pizza. A camouflaged gate opened to a little footpath down the slope toward the river. Musclewood trunks twisted upward, hickory and a few pines shaded a path, creating a tunnel of green.

We continued down the sloped path, around a few bends, to where the bent, gray, metal walls of an old warehouse and an old Lord and Burnham greenhouse crouched. All sorts of discarded mowers and tillers, the skeleton of a golf cart, and a popcorn cart with broken wheels collected leaves. On a flat spot, hundreds of potted plants stretched toward a ray of sun. No one came down here. Beyond this spot, lay a boneyard. It was literally a pit where the Animal People laid out carcasses so that beetles could clean them to bones which would later be stored for research.

Down here, everything occasionally flooded. "If the greenhouse floods, wait," Jim said. "Remember there's a zoo full of weird animals and visitors upslope. Who knows what is in all that water. For now, you're in charge of the greenhouse. It's kind of a messy mix of things we use and things waiting to move across the river."

Melodie chimed in with a half-fake, mean smile. "And now, you are in charge of the greenhouse manager. I've dealt with her for too long. Of all the existing staff, she's the only one who resents anyone stepping in as her boss."

Melodie always loved a little drama. "You'll need to hire someone experienced before the new greenhouse and growing center across the river open," Melodie continued. "She wants the job. You'll have to manage that, too."

I hadn't considered managing older and disgruntled employees, or being an outcast in a world of Animal People, or the immediate anxiety of realizing all of my duties. Suddenly, I realized I would have to face months of shuffling and nursing this mess of plants alternating with the writing of policies. There would be people to deal with. It felt like locker-room anxiety. I looked back at Mel and Jim as I asked myself, "How can you make this succeed?"

Finally, in a confident voice, I said, "Listen y'all. I can get this in order. I can identify all the plants. I can enter them into a new accession database. I can handle grumpy gardeners. But I need something besides all this cleaning up. I need something that feels new, something exciting with plants."

We started walking back and were almost at Safari Pizza, when Jim, in full boss mode, said, "You'll be designing. You'll be writing an accession policy. You'll be writing job descriptions. And by the way, you'll be coordinating the Assessment Project from the American Association of Museums. You'll be in the closet, I mean the attic, most of the time."

"But I need my hands-on stuff," I said.

Jim put his hand on his hips and slipped back into queen mode, "Tell me, Mr. Farmer. What plant can you work with, quick and easy, fast and attention-grabby, amidst all your administration duties?"

He pulled open the gate to Safari Pizza and turned back to me, "Tell me, Mr. Farmer, what will satisfy your urges?"

06: Surveying the River and New Garden Site

"Winnie," I said out loud, "we are going to ruin this for the pot smokers and teenage lovers." My loaner dog didn't respond. We had slipped between two bus-sized granite boulders, sliding down, to land in front of a cave set up with a mattress and a Piggly Wiggly cooler.

Being in the woods alone made me happy. I could think and look. The slope and the water below meant there was a huge variation in plant types. Maybe lurking in these woods would be an undiscovered, dramatic, career-building plant that I could bring into the garden trade. Maybe I would find what could become the signature plant for the Garden.

It would have to be a salvage project for sure. These woods would soon be the Garden's construction site. We were going to build something new here, something that would challenge the centuries-old, boring, eco-harmful, exclusive garden ways of the area. The South was changing, and here, in these woods, we'd illustrate this new South with new garden styles that modern people were craving.

Lots of folks were unhappy about the change. The Zoo had already put up a fence. For decades adventurous teens from town came here to camp and party. Kayakers walked around the rapids, and daredevils swam. On Sunday mornings gay guys cruised here. Rumor said Sherman slept in the cave before he burnt Columbia. Years ago I'd done all that, too. I got why people were mad about the construction, but this place was steep, slick, and inaccessible to rescuers. Simply put, it was big-time dangerous.

Under the largest pawpaw grove I had ever seen, a dozen sofa-sized boulders sat in a carpet of white variegated oak tree seedlings. I'd seen this happen ten summers in a row. One towering tree overhead dropped mutant acorns that all came up, but usually died by fall as they lacked enough chlorophyll to feed themselves.

Way on down the slope were granite walls complete with arches, the lone ruins of a Confederate uniform factory. Thigh-thick fox grape vines and waist-high dwarf palmettos clung to the moist crevices. The stone ruins, under a green cathedral, held deep, dark, clear pools with sheets of water running over flat boulders. It was a Venetian pool fantasy. I balanced on top of a wall, walking across the sluice and down.

Winnie took off, bounding toward voices up ahead. Anyone down the bank this far was probably cool. And probably handsome. Only the most athletic of folks made it this far.

The guys were built, long-haired, hippy rednecks, probably high schoolers. The red-headed one squatted, greeting Winnie and me as he said, "Boy, he's handsome and tough to come down the hill. Does he swim?"

After they offered me a smoke, which I passed on, they started going off about how the Zoo was taking over this land that had been free and public, their playground, and how now they'd have to pay. "They got roads and buildings and an amphitheater where they'll probably play Christian rock."

The redheaded guy had gray, wild eyes; burgundy jorts; and nipples the same color. "You seen the plans?"

"Yeah," I hesitated. Technically, I should have told them to leave or should have called the Zoo's security. Instead, I followed up with: "I'm the new guy, the plant guy, the one who's gonna build all that."

"What? Man, why does it have to be so closed in? The walls, the fence. What about the kayakers? It's not like you're gonna have gorillas over here. Y'all shittin' on the people."

The other one, a young Tom Petty in blue jean shorts, tried to keep mellow. "It's beautiful here, man. We have to share it. It's going to be all native plants and stuff. Right, brother?"

I was six years old again. I wanted to play with these big boys and be as easy and fun as they were. I had to lie a little bit. "The landscape architects who did the plans were from Philadelphia. There are too many walls and too many bricks. It's sort of pretentious, but that was all done before I got here. I just started. I get to nix all their hedges and English garden plants, and fill it up with good plants that love our heat."

Tom Petty smiled as he held out a flower. "Brother, do you know what kind of flower this is?"

I touched the tissue-thin petals that his bony fingers touched. "Spider Lily. Hymenocallis coronaria. It means beautiful, crowned, membrane."

The crazy-eyed redhead laughed maniacally, "Boy, I don't know about you, but I definitely understand what a hymen is." Then, as if he knew what I'd been thinking about his friend, he threw his head back and wailed the lyrics from Tom Petty's "American Girl."

Winnie had wandered off and was starting to bark like crazy. I decided to follow her barks, leaving the fellas to their smoking and swimming. These guys were at once attractive, boring, and a little scary.

I walked away and found Winnie barking by a towering buttress of what used to be the bridge into town. He looked tiny by massive granite blocks. He stared across the river, freaked out by the siamang apes howling in the woods. We were right across from the

Zoo. I could see my current office from here. The Garden side, where we stood, was rocky, clay cliffs, typical of half of Columbia. But 100 yards across the river, where the Zoo sat, was a sandy flood plain, typical of the other half of town.

Pretty soon, we would start construction on a bridge that would unite the Zoo and the Garden. The two sides of the river and the two landscapes represented a divide that you could feel throughout town.

————

Columbia sits atop an ancient geological divide. The tectonic plate that formed the Blue Ridge mountains clashed, right here where Winnie and I stood, with a plate that used to be an ancient ocean. One was a hard, mineral-rich, burgundy clay. The other a pale, crystalline, nutrient-poor sand.

Just east of town, in any of 22 active sand mines, mountains of the stuff lay like inviting sugary playgrounds. Some of the sand was so pure that it was used to make glass. On those lands, the plants and most of the people were poor.

The Sandhills' native forest looks almost like a desert. Knee-high sparse grasses hover over flat cacti. Rare dwarf pixie moss, in the same botanical order as blueberries and persimmon trees, reaches a quarter inch tall. In normal forests, trees hold their leaves horizontally so as to gain as much solar energy as possible for photosynthesis. Here it's so hot and bright that the dwarf turkey oaks evolved to hold leaves vertically, protecting themselves from sunburn. They even photosynthesize best in the morning and evening when the sun is low.

But a mile further inland, the rich red clays of the Piedmont boast towering white oaks and tulip poplar trees that cast dense shade onto sword ferns and mountain laurels. Granite boulders emerge from steep hillsides, and clear, rocky streams still invite hippy boys to swim, tube, and chill.

A few visionaries back in the late 1960s gave Columbia its first and only major tourist attraction right where these two ecotypes clashed in the distant past. Riverbanks Zoo remains the largest single tourist attraction in the entire state. It was one of only a handful of zoos that refused to use cages and pens. Lions and tigers roamed cageless in naturalistic, open-air habitats. While other zoos had flower beds and park-like settings, this one had bamboo groves along with tropical jungles and black water swamps. Jim had planted most of these areas then transferred their management to Melodie.

————

I swung by Melodie's house after my hike to announce that the hippy boys I had run into were right. "The plans are imposed on the site. All that brick. Walls."

She raked a comb through her wet hair to help the henna set in. "And the building looks like a golf course clubhouse. But you know those sorts of drawings help sell it. At least Jim sent the landscape architects packing when they tried to talk about plants."

"I saw some of their planting plans. Endless hedges. They have no idea. Boxwoods for miles in full sun. And does Jim really like all these English perennials? I've seen the Kurt Blummel Nursery invoices for truckloads of plants from that Maryland nursery. All of them are dead now."

Mel chimed in, "Every single plant in Blummel's catalog dies by August here. Loads of plants are always killed by our summer heat and sun. You and Jim get to argue through all that."

Winnie tried to hump Mel's dog Pig, the most butch bitch in the world. I'd have to get out of here soon. I was roasting oysters for Winnie's mom's party this evening anyway.

I told her, "I'm going to use a lot of your tropical perennial stuff from the Zoo. We can do as much together as you want."

"Once y'all leave the office, cross the river, you'll never ask me anything," Mel said slightly under her breath as I had started to leave.

Smiling, I turned slightly to look back at her. "Your middle-child syndrome is talking again."

Later that evening I headed over to roast oysters and take Winnie home. I'd agreed to this party only because Winnie's mom was an old friend. She was a strong, curious, and thoughtful power lesbian who lived half-time in Columbia and half-time in Madrid, Spain. She asked me to roast oysters for her party, and I said yes for two reasons. First, roasting oysters puts me in a cloud of smoke, occupies my hands and thoughts, and means I do not have to engage with people. I would be around people but unable to engage with them. Second, because she, like me, felt sort of disconnected from Columbia by her job. I liked the idea of a loose connection; a friend but without duties and expectations. She seemed to like that too.

The party sprawled around a house on a little city lot. Plywood tables, coolers, and fans made up the bulk of the furniture. Black-netted speakers as big as crates blared "Burning Down the House." Earlier, before the party, I'd dug a pit for roasting the oysters and then laid out rusty pieces of tin to cook on. Before all of that, I had planned a discreet entrance. So despite Winnie bounding through the crowd, I was able to huddle into starting a fire, getting some steam going, and prying open a few oysters to test their sliminess.

A very young lesbian couple, who looked a bit like boyish baseball players, captured my attention. "I work at the museum," one said while watching me fiddle with the oysters. "And we should do something together with the Garden."

"Sounds good to me, the Garden is really a living museum."

We bonded almost immediately. They ended up helping me sling wet burlap, spread oysters, and not be too bothered by annoying guests for the rest of the party. Then she said in a fairly drunk slurry accent, "Every Sunday morning we have a big communal breakfast. You should come. Dad would love you. I mean, would he love you?"

I just said OK as I packed up oyster knives and gloves. Time to head home. But the Uncles, wise in these things, chimed in. "Red Flag! Did you hear how she said Daddy will love you? She practically said, 'Old Daddy loves young chicken!' And that means you."

07: Liberating Pansies with Asian Veggies

The Uncles, men who came of age in the 1950s, gently taught me life lessons. You might think a gay country boy from the rural South didn't have gay Uncles, but I did. First in my life was Daddy's brother, Buist, and his lover, whom the whole family called Uncle Michael.

Then there were a host of other confirmed bachelors, garden mentors, antique dealers, and obvious-to-me "uncles." I had never wanted to be their kind of gay. They seemed pretentious, having been cowed into small defined roles. Here at the Zoo, however, I started to appreciate them, to lean on and even seek their wisdom, but it wasn't always easy.

Jim Martin, a new Southerner originally from an Ohio dairy farm, didn't have the extended "family" that I did. He appreciated these erudite uncles, the old queen crowd — the ones I sometimes took for granted. So I was happy to have them on my side during perennial border design presentations. I lacked Jim's experience so I needed backup for some of my more intuitive ideas.

Full of skepticism and empowered by authority, Jim often said, "OK. The timing sounds good. Now, show me how it works on the color wheel." The color wheel is really just a collection of unchallenged rules based on someone else's ideas of beauty. Unimaginative garden designers use it like Baptists use the Bible. As the Bronski Beat song says, "Things that you're liable to read in the Bible, they ain't necessarily so."

The uncles screamed, "Gershwin said it first in Porgy and Bess!"

Thanks y'all.

Appreciation of color combinations changes with culture, climate, and even with crazes. I wanted Jim to see beyond the accepted rules. But for the time being, I said, "I'll try to find an example," and turned away, rolling my eyes.

Why did everything have to be proven with Jim? Couldn't we, the entire creative team, be the ones to prove something? He was the boss with a great team. Why couldn't we be the ones to build a new world and ignore the old rules? I played his game.

I should just pick up the phone and call my interior designer uncle and ask him how I could show that a dark brown carex, a burgundy crinum, and warm yellow 'Autumn Minaret' daylilies work together. He would give me the goods: "You know Churchill's library was done in exactly that color palette. It may seem dark and heavy for a flower garden, but tell your boss you're inspired by that interior color palette. Add a bit of aqua blue and greens all around to keep it lively."

I ran my answers by Melodie. "Jim wanted me to justify this planting. I mean, it's going to be beautiful, right? But you know how he needs to feel like it's creative but not too far out. So this is what I'm going to say..."

"That'll work," she said, "but elaborate on the bit about English gardens."

Melodie and I learned how to frame and justify ideas. She was better at it and more patient than I was. "All you have to do is throw in something English or back up your proposal by saying you got the idea from some fancy botanical garden."

We were snarky, reverse snobs. Square pegs. I figured out really early on that if you can't be part of the team or clique, then you make your own.

If you were always the last picked for a sports team, we would definitely be friends. So while the jocks liked to be shirtless, I liked to be barefoot. Even as an acolyte at church, I'd try to do it barefoot without being caught. Obviously, I was not part of the church team either. I should have fit into the country boy crew. I drove tractors and was in charge of the hay baling process from cut to stack. But I knew I was looking at the other guys' new bits of chest and armpit hair, and that definitely wasn't part of being on their "team."

I was kind of like a chameleon, learning early on that I could fit in if I wanted. I used to go to Dairy Camp in the summer. It was a camp for dairy farmers' children. At this camp, instead of rowing and carving, we had milking, pre-vet, and breeding lessons. At the end of the week we even had a Dairy Bowl contest, patterned after TV game shows.

One summer I got to be buddies with one of the cool jock guys. To impress him, I developed a hot and heavy romance with Helen, the only girl in camp who had parental permission to smoke. Helen got whisked away daily for secret therapy sessions. People didn't talk about that sort of stuff then. At night, in the screened gathering room by the lake, most kids played board games or air hockey. Helen and I slow-danced. In an already gravelly, smoky voice, she sang the lyrics to her favorite song "The Rose."

Aside from being a chameleon, I developed a pattern that always seemed to play itself out: Get drawn in by the comfort of the crowd. Then push away from the crowd because it is the crowd.

In college one year I was briefly in the Block and Bridle club with the cowboys. That same year, I wore a pompadour, lipstick, and pearls to Intro to Ag class and for the yearbook photo. Get drawn in, then pull away.

A slight variation of my pattern was to emulate, then ridicule. I'd done that with Jim ever since we'd met in the Horticulture Club. I would participate in the trips he would arrange, complete with university buses, conference fees paid, and some free meals. Then I would make fun of him for being so much a part of the system.

Now, Jim and I had a trade-off. I needed to participate to reach my own goals. Jim needed me to play a role or at least borrow some prestige from my erudite Uncles until I developed my own. The Uncles had survived their lives by playing roles: offering lessons on culture and making themselves valuable in a public way, but hiding their love and sex lives from the public eye. One of the best at doing this happened to be one of the country's most connected and respected horticulturists: Dr. J.C. Raulston.

———

Dr. Raulston gave lectures around the world. He personally knew the elite of English gardens but also the trendsetters of Spanish, Russian, Korean, and Japanese horticulture. We had connected back in college when I had tried to do graduate work with him at North Carolina State, but he had sent me packing.

"No way," he said. "You have to leave. Go to Seattle. You'll find a whole new world of creative people, sexy gay guys, and the most amazing plants and gardens in this country. You can always come home."

Since moving back to the South, I had frequently stayed at his home in Raleigh and hung out with him at his job at North Carolina State. J.C.'s word was gold in any argument when Jim required validation.

On my next trip, I put my problem to J.C. like this: "I can manage the current plants and the designs, but I don't know how to satisfy Jim. How can I set a plant agenda with immediate results and a long-term run? He's queeny and petty sometimes. Now, he's making me grow out all the pansies for the Zoo. It's going to look like someone threw a quilt on the ground, complete with a fringe of peacock kale puffs." I watched while J.C. shuffled slides across a light table, flipping them into carousels for next week's lectures. This was my crash course: Plants and Gardens of the World through the Lens of J.C. Raulston.

"Get your own databases up and running," he told me. "I track twenty thousand slides and all the plants in the Arboretum. And look at this one," he said with a smirk as he held up a slide of a curly-haired gardener showing off his "equipment."

"I met this handsome gardener in Spain, and he was not shy."

Like most of the Uncles, he'd spent decades diligently filing personal life separately from professional.

———

In the frosty morning light, we would go through his arboretum nursery where diversity ruled, messy and beautiful.

J.C. would chatter in that stream-of-consciousness way of his. "You should take these restios. They're from South Africa and will grow better in your zone. Can you go to South Africa with me next spring? Here, take one of each of these, but don't record where they came from."

I took everything he offered, but I couldn't take in and remember his overwhelming stream of details. I ran a microcassette recorder when we loaded plants.

"I don't know why someone grew this Japanese apricot from seed," he said as he pulled out a dozen wimpy one-gallons. "I should throw them away." But he couldn't. He didn't have a family. He had his plants. They had become his world when he was an isolated, ostracized gay boy in 1950s Oklahoma. In later years, J.C. would recall, "As a boy, I played with plants because I knew they wouldn't hurt me."

He nested a small, broken apricot tree into my pickup cab. Even that couldn't be left behind. The back of the truck was overflowing as I drove down the interstate. Suddenly, the tailgate banged open. Twenty rare white cedars, fifteen Afrocarpus trees, and eleven Japanese apricots smashed onto I-95. The sole survivor was the decapitated Japanese apricot tree in the cab. It eventually got planted in Riverbanks' Winter Garden, where its early-in-life trauma made it grow a wild and sprawling branch pattern that later turned into sculptural trunks.

"Help people see beauty where they've never seen beauty before," J.C. told me.

We used to stop at the White Rabbit, a gay book store where everybody knew his name, and he would point me to the best new fiction. I appreciated his lessons. All the Uncles wanted to make young men more culturally literate. I appreciated J.C.'s lessons in literature and all the gay bookstore chatchka, but at the moment those things were distractions. I was anxious to get J.C. back to discussions focused on solving my plant dilemma.

Back in J.C.'s cocoon — a converted warehouse with black ceilings, books, and art on every wall — I could finally push the conversation. He'd been thinking about it and told me, "I can grow odd stuff up here in relative isolation. But you and Jim have to please people. And you have to please Jim. Remember when we went to the premiere of Priscilla Queen of the Desert in Seattle? Afterward you walked me through the Asian community garden and showed me all those colorful Asian greens you loved. They're all the same plant as collards, turnips, and mustard greens — Southern staples that thrive all winter in your climate. Do them."

He gave me a midnight massage, and then I went to bed to drift off into a kaleidoscope dream of Seattle fog, purple mustard, glossy tatsoi. I woke up with the words that would become my mantra. Liberate the pansies.

———

I knew that to liberate the pansies, so to speak, I would need the help of greenhouse manager Kathy Kovac, a salt-of-the-earth country woman five or six years older than I was and suspicious of my new-fangled ideas. I'd been made her manager, and she resented me. In the face of any new idea, she made her bangs fall over her face, then cut her eyes through the curtain of hair, harumph, and start dreaming up ways to sabotage the idea. At times, she didn't say anything outright, but I could read the thought in her eyes. "Granny did it this way, and that ought to be good enough for us."

I tried a novel approach with her this time. "Jim thinks this is a terrible idea. He says collards are shack plants for poor people and white trash, and they will never be beautiful enough for his gardens."

The Uncles loved this approach and quoted Churchill — they loved him, too — to show their approval. "Now that we are linked in righteous comradeship...."

But we were not quite linked, Kathy and I. She presented every possible scenario of failure. At last, she said, "There's not enough sun in this greenhouse."

She was right. This greenhouse was shaded by hickory trees. Now, I got the chance to prove my commitment, to solve a problem she'd come up with, and to show that I valued her experience. I commandeered space behind the tiger exhibit, a prominent backstage spot that all the animal people went through daily. I chose it for its sun, a hose bib, and its provocative position. I sent a memo explaining what Kathy was doing. We were linked now, and she was getting well-deserved credit. It proved to be a winning approach as Kathy produced flat after flat of purple mustards, golden mizuna, rainbow chard, and red kale—all perfectly timed for October planting.

The main trial area was an abandoned plot between Public Restroom Two and the Reptile People's smoking area. Kyle, an Ohio redneck, watched. I started timing my veggie work with his breaks, and he started taking me out snake hunting at dusk. I did have a little crush.

Melodie rolled her eyes. "You have a boyfriend in Seattle."

"You're so conventional," I said, knowing that would offend her. "I'm more of a love-the-one-you're-with kind of guy."

She rolled her eyes again. "Wasting your time. You're wasting your time. He is an Ohio redneck. I bet he's slept with every bird keeper and her sister."

Banter aside, Melodie always made magic with whatever plants I sent her way. She mixed Asian greens with her regular pansy and bulb schemes.

By spring, around the Flamingo Gift Shop, orange sherbet tulips swayed among burgundy mustard leaves. In the whisky barrels around Kenya Cafe, lacquered, kelly green tatsoi rubbed against pale blue pansies. Waist-high, orange-stem Swiss chard at the entry to our drab attic office became an easy microwavable lunch.

We documented production schedules, frost responses, rabbit preferences, and color combinations. We took sexy photos. Slides were neatly filed and described in Riverbanks' Filemaker database, which was a direct copy of J.C.'s database. Finally, we were confident and ready to invite the press to the Garden to celebrate and promote these cool new plantings and tease the public with a taste of what the celebrated new Botanical Garden would do.

Jim used his extensive network to make a coming-out plan. Color photos and promos ran in the newspaper, and whetted the public's appetite for these new plants. The city committed to hundreds of veggie flats for fall. A commitment like that made it profitable for wholesale nurseries to grow our unusual plants, which meant homeowners would be able to buy them, too. Columbia was soon blanketed in purple mustard, chartreuse mizuna, red Russian kale, crinkly parsley, and glossy tatsoi. Suddenly, the old boring palette of pansies and peacock kale had a whole new level of texture, color, and height.

Jim continued to do his magic on TV and in slide lectures. We were doing what the Garden was meant to do: stimulate the local horticulture industry. Homeowners got cool new plants, nurseries made money, and we got accolades. Even from afar. The concept wasn't new. A few creative individual gardeners had been doing it for years, but we got to do it on a grand scale, to test the boundaries, to popularize more and more veggies, and to showcase greens as winter garden plants. We shared information with other gardens, too. The next year, the first International Flower Show at EPCOT featured veggies.

But our new movement needed some research that only a university could carry out. While I could show pretty slide shows all day long, the growers and the retail industry needed details like growth rate, pest controls, soil types, even growth hormone research. We lacked connections, and J.C. helped. He asked me to do my "Liberate Your Pansies" lecture in Raleigh. Afterwards, a young graduate student approached me. He was looking for research trials focused on commercial nursery production. During my lecture, he saw an opportunity for doctoral research. That young man spent the next few years doing much needed research that brought these Asian veggie plants to a wider audience. He continued that research even after he became a professor—Dr. James Gibson at the University of Florida.

On the heels of this success, Jim Martin and others seemed to buy into my vision a bit more. It made sense to work with plants that had a Southern history or at least were relatives that thrive in our climate. The same went for design. Looking to places like Britain or Philadelphia for inspiration would always lead to failure. No need to rehash or glorify the past. We needed to look to the Caribbean, Florida, and even Mexico. We wanted to change the usual approach. Rather than focusing on temperature, rain patterns, and soils, we changed the focus to sun intensity, breezes, shade, and timing to enhance people's enjoyment of the space.

I was putting all this on paper late one night at my house when Jim pulled up. We sat on my little porch with a fire and the house lights out. He opened up about his current relationship. Jim thought he'd finally found love. He and the new man in his life had practically moved in together. But it just wasn't working out. Jim wondered out loud, "We just don't fit. It's like he's totally focused on being gay. It's just not going to work out."

Though he was sad, this seemed like more relief than pain for him. He'd come over to my bohemian oasis to slum. To let it out. To relax. Candles burned inside and turmeric curtains fluttered in the window. All I could do was offer a bit of physical comfort. We found a camaraderie that night. Respect. Maybe a bit of pent-up emotion got released. Right there on the dark deck, we found more. I didn't last eight minutes. He left a bit embarrassed.

I went to bed thinking I should write a letter to Kevin, a world away in Seattle, to see where things stood with us.

As I was falling asleep, I began to recall my fantasy. Could Jim and I be like buddies who loved plants and each other? The gay garden power couple of Tighty Whitey Town? Huck Finn and Tom Sawyer, collecting plants in the swamps, mixing them in our gardens, breaking rules? I could see the couple's pic on the cover of Southern Living, and smiled as I drifted off to sleep.

The Uncles cackled in my head, waking me up.

"Child, there wasn't eight of anything in that room. Not inches, not minutes. That was two horny guys and a release of a lot of frustration. Nothing wrong with that. Y'all both doing good, letting old expectations slip away. Say goodbye to Seattle. Quit writing all the time. Open up. Liberate some more pansies."

The Uncles loved a good double entendre.

08: Ladies Touring the Garden Construction Site

The growing crew we had hired in early summer elected to work "tropical hours" for the rest of the season so that we could go home before the real heat of the afternoon. We started at 6 a.m. On these hot mornings folks slid in sporadically around six o'clock. Only three were true morning people. Tommy Cave (our part-time tool man who had retired from the prison system) was not one of them. He told me flatly, "Son, give it a few decades, and you'll understand how it takes longer and longer to get cranked up in the mornings."

Standing beside me in the work bay just before six on that first morning of "tropical hours" was my carpool pal — Good Old Girl in Overalls (GOGO). We had carpooled together with big cups of coffee and muffins she had made. Glancing at the clock, we wondered who else would show up on time.

Suddenly our youngest guy on the crew cruised in. Surprisingly he was also a morning person. He wore carharts™ and oyster roast t-shirts all summer. Blond and blue-eyed, he looked like a college baseball player that young girls would chase for his autograph. I'm pretty sure some days he came straight from a frat bar in Five Points. I called him Tractor Boy or sometimes GOTBY, which was short for Good Ole Tractor Boy.

On this particular day, per usual, GOTBY never said a word. He just tipped his Ray-Bans™ slightly, buddy punched me in the chest, and clambered up onto the front-end loader. He got right to business and quickly cranked it up, engaged the tracks, and rolled out to the Garden construction site.

GOGO pointed to a box of three plastic baby doll heads, several flip-flops, and a few crushed malt liquor cans. She hooked thumbs on her overall straps, poked her stomach out a bit, and let out a cynical conversation starter: "That's some top quality compost you're getting us." A very experienced gardener, GOGO knew compost, and her cynicism was warranted.

"That's the city stuff," I countered. "We've honestly bought up all the compost available in town. We've cleaned out the horse breeder from Camden, and the monks who raised chickens near Charleston are driving up from the abbey with their last truck of compost today."

There was a look of concern on GOGO's face now. So I told her the partly good news and partly not-so-good news: "Next week I have four semis coming straight from a commercial egg farm. The guy warned me that it's a little hot. And there will be carcasses in it."

GOGO put both hands on her hips and threw her head back, making her fox-fluffy, gray ponytail cascade as she said, "I might have a carcass to add by then." She locked a menacing gaze on me, grinned, and then broke into her signature maniacal laugh that always made me laugh, too, wondering if she was having a fit.

"And I'm sure no one would ever suspect you, Lizzie Borden," I told her.

With the whole quirky cast of characters gathered, minus GOTBY, questions flew. I had unspoken acronyms for them all.

GOGO asked, "Can I have your Zoo credit card for tractor fuel?"

OBG (only Black guy) said, "What time does the Pope's poop truck come?"

Bren/Brenda asked, "Do we have volunteers today?"

OBG2 (only Brazilian guy) took us all totally off track when he yelled to the plant records keeper, "Jordan! Why are you on crutches?"

With work carts loaded, questions answered, and more coffee poured, the crew zipped their work carts out of the tractor bay. There was always one that backfired halfway up the construction road. It did not disappoint this morning. Hearing it made me smile.

––––––

If you looked up the road, you'd see that it ran under a tunnel of trees and up the west side of a hill. That hill did a good job of blocking out the sun as it rose. But heading further up the hill, you came to a sharp curve that ripped the roof off the tunnel of trees. There, at the top of that hill, was a huge oak tree with chairs under it. It was our break spot.

Under the shade of that oak tree we could survey the entire Garden construction site, an expanse of red clay, gravel paths, partially laid brick walkways, and the faux antebellum-golf-course-clubhouse-looking shell of the Visitors Center.

This morning the site was already buzzing with construction workers.

As we drove our work carts to the crest of the hill, we all stopped at the shade tree. It was a chance to smoke that one last cigarette and take that one last sip of coffee. A year ago this spot was a small pet cemetery, with a few swings hanging under a massive white oak.

I said my boss-bit, laying out how the typical late summer day would unfold — a back-and-forth of moving compost, taking breaks, and dealing with interruptions for tours or press.

"Let's get the fruit and berry garden finished up today, y'all. Tomorrow, we can plant all the citrus trees. Around ten y'all keep your eyes out for the compost truck from the chicken farm monastery. I think Brother Stan is driving it today. And at nine Jim and

I have to meet with and give a tour to five Garden Club state officers. These are big donors. The Big Bosses will be here to say hey, but Jim and I will lead the tour to the river wildflower trail."

Everybody groaned as I continued, "We told them to wear sneakers for the hike down to the river. Fellas, put your shirts on when you see them."

GOGO let loose her biggest and fakest you-are-an-idiot guffaw. Then she said, "I hope you have a backup plan because those ladies are meeting here to show off their shoes. I don't care what you told them. They ain't wearing brogans or high tops. These ladies will be dressed to impress. You'll be carrying them out of that ravine. Mark my words."

Her words lingered for a moment in the building humidity of the morning, as everyone went to their stations and started the compost-moving routine. We were a well-oiled machine. GOTBY would scoop up bucket loads of compost from his throne on the tractor, which was set up by a mountain of compost where the semis unloaded. The drivers on our crew would line up to pull their carts under his bucket. One would zip away, carefully maneuvering through construction obstacles and into the Garden, where the ground crew shoveled the compost out of the cart. Round and round it all would continue, punctuated by a short break followed by more of the same thing until two.

Three sweaty months of this quickly filtered out any new gardener who was not a true believer in the cause or who didn't fit into this irreverent and no-nonsense crew.

At eight-fifty this morning, Jim and the Admin crew pulled up in the zebra van and stopped at our pet cemetery break spot under the shade tree. They got out and immediately started to set up chairs, a poster easel, and a water cooler near the giant wood chip pile.

Jim looked over at me and lamented. "I tried to put them off until October." But at nine on the dot the ladies arrived, all at once, so that we saw ten sensible sandals stepping out of three gleaming Acuras. No sneakers.

I noticed all the guys put their shirts on as Jim walked over and greeted the women, immediately launching into his introduction to the progress in this area.

"Y'all remember just a few months ago, we met right here with this same artist's drawing and a dream? Right where we stand today. But on that cool day, if you remember, this spot was still a pet cemetery! With your support, look at how the Garden is growing!"

By nine-thirty we had ushered the tour group through the construction and down the slope, first to the site of a soon-to-be wildflower meadow, then to an overlook to see the ruins of the mills. The footpath led us through waist-high vegetation and dark forest. It wasn't an easy trek. We helped the ladies down the boulder-strewn slope to a beautiful little beach at the river's edge — the same place I had met teenage Tom Petty on one of my first days of work.

It was lovely, and the ladies were enjoying themselves. But Jim gave me a we've-made-a-colossal-mistake look. Sensible sandals would never get some of these ladies back up the slope. Trying to avert catastrophe, we quickly called for some of the compost haulers to clean off their cart seats and drive as far down the river slope as they could. Once they were in place, Jim and I would help the ladies up to the rescue point.

I had never met the state garden club president. I didn't even know her name, though that's not unusual, since at the time it was appropriate for a proper Southern lady to use her husband's name on any kind of envelope. I knew the president only as Mrs. Lucian Pope Stephens.

On the ride Mrs. Lucian Pope Stephens was clinging to my shoulder like a plane crash victim. But she was laughing at the predicament and carrying on the whole time she was being "rescued." We stopped to rest once, and she hugged me like a long lost son.

"I'm Emily," she said. "My husband loved the land." She took a breath and smiled. "He tried to farm and worked in tobacco. But in the sixties he ended up with a motel in Myrtle Beach. And Katy bar the door, we never looked back! We had such an adventure running that little motel. I'm not afraid of adventure. This hike was partly my idea."

I tried to make conversation, but it was all stilted at best. "I'm so glad you had the idea to have this little adventure. It may have turned out to be a bit more adventure than y'all bargained for, but it will make a good story down the road."

"It's a hoot! Thank you for carrying my Nine Wests in your pockets. But my panty hose will still be ruined!"

I smiled as I reflected on three things I learned that day. First, I learned that Nine Wests are shoes; second, I learned that Emily had a keen sense of fashion; and third, I learned that she was observant, which became obvious with her next question.

She asked, 'Do you have a roommate?"

I shook my head.

"I should bring my son to see the Garden soon. Y'all two would like each other. Listen to an old lady. Don't let time slip up on you while you're all consumed with this Garden. You wait too long, and you will never be able to know how wonderful a life with the same person can be, even when it changes course in crazy ways."

I smiled but I was quiet for a while. She'd told me this romantic little story, and I felt hollow in the pit of my stomach. What had I done? Had I blown the only chance for that kind of love.

I'm pretty sure that was the first time in my life that an older, pearl-wearing, church-going Southern lady didn't ask if I had a girlfriend or wanted me to meet her granddaughter.

Finally, having crossed the glaring construction site and back in the shade of the tree break site, we were exhausted and recovered with cold grapes and jugs of tea. It was the perfect finish for that part of the tour. And we all had GOGO to thank for it. Her foresight into how our little adventure might end had led her to making a quick trip to the store for the perfect wrap-up to our little adventure. I loved this crew.

After the tour had left, Jim tried to wrap up the day. "This is exactly the sort of team bonding that is making this Garden ours!"

He might as well have said, "There is no I in team," because no one was listening. Instead, we were loving watching GOTBY glistening in the sun, as he continued to unload the monks' compost. His performance was athletic and engrossing. There's something almost erotic about watching a person who's going through motions in such a competent way. The tractor pirouetted, compost flowed, and blond curls caught the breeze. GOTBY knew he was the star of a show. He could have opened a diet Coke, brushed his forearm to his brow, and been in the TV commercial, too.

Then it happened.

Either his cockiness caught up to him or maybe his Ray-Bans™ blurred something, but he made a mistake. A big one. His bucket, full of a heaping tractor scoop full of what we all called Pope's Poo, rose over the tractor, and instead of dumping its load, it kept right on going until it tilted. At first, it was just a little halo of chicken manure dust. Then things started to go in slow-motion as he mouthed, "Sumbitch."

He knew it was too late. We all knew it was too late. The bucket didn't stop. And GOTBY's confidence drained away as that too-high tractor scoop dumped a cubic yard of compost right on his head. Blond, sweaty curls were drenched in clumps of black chicken manure as little white streaks of Pope poo melted down his biceps.

GOTBY jumped to the ground, peeled off his shirt, and started wiping the manure off his chest. As it became apparent that GOTBY was OK, we all noticed the guests, being proper Southern ladies and here in an official capacity, stifling their laughter.

The other guys knew this sort of little thing could still turn serious. They ran out to him and, most importantly, stabilized the tractor. I kept my place but swelled with pride.

There's nothing like a few months of hard-working monotony and shared vision to bond a crew.

Mrs. Lucian Pope Stephens said, "You all must have been working together for a very long time." I thought I even saw a bit of pride in her eye as she asked, "You all really care, don't you?"

I didn't correct her on the time frame. "Emily, we have the best crew from the boss down."

The compost-moving tractors cranked back up, and a figure from the truck headed toward us — Brother Stan, the monastery's delivery monk. He wasn't the typical compost truck driver, nor was he anything at all like the monks I'd known in my Catholic school days. He dressed like any middle-aged, bearded gardener in Birkenstocks, though he was a bit of a salesman.

"Ladies, I feel partially responsible for what you just saw since that is our compost, straight from Mepkin Abbey. But I can assure you that it is top-quality compost from our best-laying girls. Come fall, we'll be selling gift bags of Monastery compost in local garden centers. I have one for each of you. I hope you'll tell your friends about this day!"

Brother Stan had delivered compost to us for months now. He often stayed for breaks, lunch, and sometimes offered me sage advice about life, all couched in compost or garden tales. The crew called him the sales monk, but Brother Stan had become a true friend and advisor to me. Given that I had no fondness for any of the religions I'd been exposed to, this was a big surprise.

One previous afternoon, I complained to Brother Stan that this life of mine in its singular focus on plants, both at home and work, sometimes made me feel like I needed a diversion. Maybe I needed to learn to play the guitar or learn to salsa or develop a more robust social life.

"Jenks." he said, "You need to realize that lots of people come into the monastery seeking stability, vowing themselves not only to a place but to a way of life that supports a singular focus. There is wisdom in that kind of stability. It creates the kind of ground that allows for roots to grow deeply and withstand trials and tribulations, but also to feed a passion for a particular kind of life."

A silence opened up between us for a moment as I let his words wash over me. My life was particular, that was true. But it didn't feel stable, especially with my relationship with Kevin or with the South. I looked up at Brother Stan, and he immediately picked up on the confusion swirling around in my head, in my heart.

"Look at it this way, Jenks. You're with the people you love all day long. You're with your plants and your passion all day. You go home and continue with your gardening passion. You have developed a type of stability in life. And if you stay with it, you'll see that this stability of life will be a life-saving anchor for you. Try not to get scared and let the world lure you into giving up on stability."

All of that sounded really good, but I knew I hadn't told him one important thing — the instability in my relationship with Kevin. So was his advice truly valid for me?

————

As the day wrapped up, the Uncles had their own particular perspective and commentary on how things had unfolded. While adjusting ascots and leather collars, they started to preach.

"Look at yourself. Befriending blue-haired garden clubbers. That lady could have been your vacation bible school teacher, the one you've held a 20-year grudge against. Now those garden club ladies would arm themselves with pruning shears to protect you. Tonight they'll mail in big checks. Your crew loves you and loves each other — rednecks, prison guards, and even that crazy cackling Southern Party Girl in bib overalls (GOGO). Every single one of them treats you more like a brother or a daddy than a boss. Look at you. You're actually doing it. You're actually settling back into the South on your own terms."

I knew there'd be some Tennessee Williams' quote coming next from them, so I tried to turn the conversation in my head. "This is fun, but y'all know how things really are. Kevin's waiting for me. I'm not setting down roots here."

They rolled their eyes indicating willful ignorance on my part to accept what was happening. In exaggerated Southern hysterical voices, they said in unison, "But you are Blanche! You are!"

09: Suddenly Single

It wasn't a voice, but a feeling that seemed to suggest words and a will of its own. I was barely awake when I heard it:

Don't open your eyes yet. Don't wake. Stay in the dark comfort, that childhood moment at dawn, safe from any hurt. Stay in bed just a few minutes more.

I was sleeping, covered by a grandmother's quilt, and alone in my new place—an artsy, cozy, hidden house covered with vines. A wave of brain freeze rolled inside my forehead, through my sinus cavities, and down into my throat. *Don't think about it. Don't think about his words. Don't wake. Sleep a little more.*

Then a voice. His voice. Kevin's words that I'd read in his letter. *"I tried, Jenks. I tried to span the miles and hours and flights. I tried waiting. But I've come too far out here. I ran away from all that oppression, and I can't go back into it. Not even for you."*

His voice in my head woke me up. It took me back to his letter, which had arrived from Seattle a week ago. As I read it, one line hit home and hurt most: "I feel like you left me. For a job."

Every morning since, I had awakened to deep loneliness and guilt.

I was officially single. Officially on my own. Besides the loss of love, I'd lost one of the things that made being here seem safe and temporary — the anchor who would have drawn me back to Seattle had our connection remained intact.

This morning I wanted to stay on my futon. There was no phone here. No interruptions. No one I'd have to tell about the letter or what it said. No one who would try to make me talk through it. Again.

Today was also a tough day to face a group. I had to present at the American Legion log cabin. I already resented these people and had put them into a box. They didn't care about plants. And they probably would not accept the real me. They probably were Sunday school teacher types with rigid rules for their club. But the truth was, I didn't even know who *they* were. I was judging them based on a stereotype, the very thing that made me run away from South Carolina.

Driving here from Seattle with Robert, who was now firmly a part of the Uncles, I'd come up with a manifesto for living here:

◊ My gardening would focus on plants, earth, soul, and art, without being influenced by the past, pesticides, and pretense.

◊ I would live as an out gay man.

◊ I would never wear the ubiquitous uniform of proper young Southern preppy men.

◊ No blue blazer, no Weejuns, nor pretentious boat shoes, and never a tie.

Kevin's letter eroded my resolve in that manifesto. It announced that I was now without my anchor.

I never thought I would be single again, but here I was. Single. Drifting around untethered in my head, yet unable to will myself out of bed. Could I have done anything differently? My mind went to surface excuses like Kevin hated the heat. Then more serious thoughts of how he hated the stratification of Southern society filled my mind. We both hated the stratification.

That cold truth started me spinning. Even among all my new garden acquaintances, there was an unspoken separation. They came together as volunteers in the Zoo. Bankers, soldiers, teachers, and housewives made smooth conversation while planting, but there were cracks in the bond of their words. The garden club ladies with golf course husbands, the military crowd, and the textile mill folks just didn't mix. Economics, education, world views, and social barriers held strong sway over each group from different perspectives. It didn't seem to matter which group. The separation ran too deep. Maybe I needed to cut this whole experiment short, go back to Seattle, and try to fix things with Kevin.

Of course, as is the usual case with life, exceptions were starting to develop. One such exception was a sense of belonging that came with the house where I was sleeping now. Porter—my most serious, most dedicated new garden volunteer and now my landlord—had told me, "I bought Willie's house when he died. I couldn't let his plants and his memory get turned into a strip mall. No one loved it. No one understood. Until you."

Porter came from salt-of-the-earth, mill-village folks. An odd duck, he'd found gardening through hobby. He'd been a teacher, and then a school administrator, and through it all, a bachelor. Gardening was an acceptable creative outlet for Southern bachelors.

"But Willie changed me," he said. "Taught me botanical Latin. If I used a common name, he'd purse his lips and pretend he hadn't heard a word."

Porter told me that once he decided to preserve Willie's home, he thought he might not be able to let anyone live in it. He said, "Even the city told me to bulldoze it. But technically, it's not in the city. Then you came along."

This connection to the old gardeners helped me formulate a plan. I'd get through this by doing what Willie had done. After Zoo and Garden obligations, I'd work on Willie's house and garden. I would spend the heat of the afternoon accessioning slides and writing. Then at dusk, I'd head out to work alone in the jungle of plants left in the yard of the once-famous TV gardener, Willie Freeland.

Gardening, or just being with plants, had always been my escape. My own private world. In the 1970s I had escaped from farm-boy pressures into the swamp, where spring-fed water flowed crystal clear under the deep magnolia shade. I made my oasis there. I used sticks, rocks, and mud for a little dam that caused a wide spot in the creek — a clear pool just big enough to submerge myself, drop my rear end into the water, and soak with head and feet up. I would gaze into the sky and dream of climbing, flying, just flat-out escaping through smooth black tree trunks. On the bank, I would move hay-scented ferns, wild ginger, and moss into nooks of black roots. I had spent hours, even years, on cold and hot days creating, daydreaming, escaping from the South.

Now, as an adult, I still found that zone while gardening alone. Squatting, peering into a tiny world, starting with black grit on thick fingers and white fleshy tubers hiding a gray earthworm, then moving beyond into a clear colorful vision of how all these things would grow, weave, and blossom together.

Doing it for money came with less peaceful duties. People. So many volunteers with their excited chatter and eager minds and many needs. Lots of them wanted something from me — to see my quiet vision, to learn a new plant, to get a cutting. They came here to escape something. Some of them wanted to talk about a recently lost spouse, an abusive husband, or a move from Milwaukee. They needed connections.

Porter was one of those who needed something. Maybe a sense of direction. Maybe more. I wasn't sure what yet. I wouldn't find out for a long time.

One day he was telling all the volunteers about my work on Willie's house. Quiet-as-a-mouse volunteer Betty Dozier suddenly clapped her hands. Under her gray perm, her eyes got wide. She broke into a huge smile, "You live in Willie Freeland's house? I thought they tore that down!" Then she clapped again and said, "That means we are neighbors!"

———

I'd never thought about who might be beyond the protective grove of bamboo and chain link that enclosed my wild, little utopia. I knew I wasn't isolated; I could hear the traffic on Rosewood and rumbling explosions from the bomb training range. Blocks away, there was a guarded gate into 53,000 acres of Sandhills forest, barracks, basic training combat courses, and rifle ranges. Ten thousand people lived, worked, and soldiered at Fort Jackson. Like me, though, they stayed in their own world behind the gates, behind that pine tree curtain that surrounded the fort.

For a while, I resisted letting my two worlds intersect. Would this sweet, older lady, this military woman, be a bother? Would she invite me to church, want me to meet her daughters, or recruit me to join a book club to discuss inspirational novels? I didn't want to lose my solitude. Now, without my distant anchor of Kevin, I feared developing connections that may push me back into the Southern tradition of "playing the part." I did not want to put myself in a situation that would betray my manifesto. I did not want to make connections that may make my planned departure difficult.

But Betty and Porter seemed safe enough, not requiring the development of deep connections. They both had intriguing links to my current house and garden, and they were convenient. Betty was just next door, and Porter was eager to stop by any chance he got. The hitch was that both were old-school, Southern types. I was afraid they'd expect me to play a certain role, to be in the closet. I also suspected that Porter was a "latent homosexual," as would have been said back in the day. I was certainly not interested in being part of that world. But he definitely had a ton of great plant connections. Betty, on the other hand, was the TV-perfect, church-going, sewing-circle housewife. She seemed to want to pull me in also.

I wanted to continue my routine —to write and garden at night, and to use my fascinating backyard (Willie's backyard) as my escape from having to play a particular role for people. But, to be honest, Betty and Porter somewhat intrigued me. I wanted to know why they were interested in me.

❧

10: Befriending the Military Widow

The house I had rented from Porter was near the fort. A belt of pine trees hid that world. In my backyard, a thicket of bamboo separated me from the neighbor Betty Dozier. It appeared that our worlds were destined to intersect.

Betty had spent her life in the military world. Her father-in-law, a decorated veteran of World War I and Adjutant General of South Carolina, rebuilt the South Carolina National Guard. His son — Betty's husband, Colonel James Charles Dozier — spent his decades-long career with the National Guard.

She lived and breathed the Army. Back in the 1950s, Betty and her sister had put on dance shows for World War II active-duty military personnel through the United Service Organization charity. She once told me, "The USO was right where Finlay Park is now. Next door, on Assembly Street, soldiers on leave for the weekend got a room at the Downtowner Motel."

It wasn't just her husband's family that had pulled Betty into the army world. Her brother had come back from World War II psychologically damaged and lived a tormented life in a Veterans Administration hospital in Dublin, Georgia. She made the three-hour trip to visit every month. Betty's commitment to her brother became a vocation to try to brighten soldiers' lives.

In the 1960s on Saturday nights at the new USO, Betty and her two teenage daughters danced with well-mannered soldiers: the ones who chose this entertainment over going to bars. Homesick new recruits joined the Dozier family for lunch on Sundays. One fellow from Boston even went on a summer family vacation with them. The family, their home, and their time served in part as a colonel's way to share and show success. Betty's job as an officer's wife was occasionally public, but she was more comfortable behind the scenes, making a lovely home and family for the colonel to share with his guests, helping him put his best foot forward.

Betty had a hot lunch ready for her husband most days. She would stand at the door, watch his car enter the winding drive and ease between the azalea hedges. Then she would rush to get hot food set on the table for his 30-minute lunch. Her girls came home later to chocolate chip cookies, milk, and Dark Shadows while she prepared a family supper to serve on the little table in the perfectly organized galley kitchen.

"But! But!," she laughed. Betty had a sweet way of laughing as she held up a finger as a signal to wait. "He might just call at two on any given afternoon or at any minute, for that matter, to say he was bringing over nine guests from Seoul or Cincinnati. I had to be organized. I had to be able to set up a reception and dinner in a few hours. I had to be able to get the girls and myself dressed for guests at the drop of a hat. That is really why my kitchen is so organized and stocked."

When her husband retired, Betty wanted to go back to school. "But he was at home, feeling the impact of health issues, and simply couldn't understand why being his wife was not enough."

He wanted her close, so she stayed close. She ended up spending a decade caring for Colonel Dozier as his health declined in his last years. After his death, her girls were still close by, but suddenly Betty was alone. She could have immersed herself as a VIP in fort life or joined the lady's clubs at Shandon Presbyterian Church. Neither was what she needed.

Each morning at five-thirty, she watched Susan Audé Fisher on Good Morning Columbia. On one particular morning, Betty turned on the television to hear, "My guest this morning is Jim Martin! He's made Columbia's zoo a wild walk through the jungles. Now he's planting 70 acres of flowers for the city!"

Jim secretly rolled his eyes but joined right in with enthusiasm, "Let's go ahead and look at these spectacular flowers! Oh my gosh, Susan, you and everyone needs a Joe Pye weed! Our beautiful yellow swallowtails love it! Y'all come on out and be part of it all. We need volunteers to plant the new garden! You might need an extra manicure, but dirt under your nails is worth being part of Columbia's garden legacy! Isn't that right, Susan?"

Handsome, confident, trustworthy Jim offered new adventure, connection to the earth, and everything Betty craved. She needed this part of grieving, to step out, to be with young people, to be outside, in a different world. She needed to reinvent herself.

Betty leapt at the chance. Volunteering got her out into the world again. She worked in the new Greenhouse and Growing Center, which would become the plant production center for Riverbanks Zoo and Garden. It was on the far side of the river from the Zoo and would eventually become the staff gateway to the garden. This facility would be managed by the third person of our crew, Jack Sustic.

———

Jack came down from Michigan State's Beaumont Nursery to interview. His just-out-of-the-army look topped off with a jet-black crewcut scared me. Jack wore a black suit every day despite the broiling South Carolina heat. I was skeptical that he'd fit in and skeptical of whom he'd bring on board when he proclaimed, "What I'm really excited about is getting to hire my own crew. The nursery where I work now is full of older, stuck-in-their-ways people. Before that, in the army, I worked with people I was assigned with."

We would be sharing not only a collection of plants but also an office. I was afraid that being ex-Army, Jack would hire rigid folks who would clash with the young creative crew I wanted. Months later, at hiring time, Jack introduced me to a hippie chick named Jennifer Glass. She was a privileged New Yorker who was a self-proclaimed plant lover. But like so many of her kind, she had not yet touched a plant. Next, he brought on hippy Keith, complete with a ponytail, John Lennon wire-rimmed glasses, and a love for magic potions that added positive neurons to plants to make them happier and "more communicative."

I rolled my eyes and balked at Jack's choices. Jack didn't need help being communicative. Always efficient but never curt in his actions or words, he just looked me in the eye and said, "You hiring? I thought I was in charge of hiring my crew."

Jack hired his crew. They talked a lot. Loudly. They played endless amounts of Grateful Dead. Loudly.

Before I got to know Betty and Jack, I'd have put military folks into a single box characterized by hyper-rigidity. But I quickly found out that I would need to rethink my profiling of these two.

I started helping Betty in her yard on some afternoons. We would work and chat till dusk. She'd have supper ready, the table set, and even a fresh t-shirt for me. Sometimes, we would eat together at her kitchen table. Other times we got comfy in upholstered swivel rockers and watched Jeopardy while eating on TV trays. Some days, Betty would even realize that I needed my quiet time and packed me a meal in tin foil pans to take with me.

Betty became my Columbia mom, and I was the gay son she never had.

She hadn't told her daughters about her new life at the Garden or me. She loved how she had constructed her world and wasn't quite ready to merge her new friends with her family. I think she loved how she got to define herself with us without any concerns of the past.

Eventually, I unknowingly spilled the beans when I met one of her daughters in a planning meeting. One of my new work duties included working with the University of South Carolina to co-host a summer lecture series. My designated contact, Tibby Dozier Steedly, was surprised but thrilled. "Mom volunteers with you?" She raised her voice in excitement just like Betty did. I realized at that moment that Betty was volunteering with us but hadn't told her family.

Betty had been secretly stepping out of her world to be with us. We were helping her make a long-desired transformation into a life of her own.

Now, she wanted to show us a part of Columbia we didn't know.

To introduce her daughters to her Garden family, Betty planned a big formal dinner: "Everyone is invited! Everyone can bring a friend or their wife or husband or roommate. We'll all dress up!"

Betty not only cooked but also served us on china plates with the silverware and even place cards. Most of our crew had never been invited to an event where they were expected to dress up.

We were a new crowd at the kind of formal dinner party that Betty could execute perfectly with her eyes closed. But this would not be our only dinner invitation from Betty. Later, Betty took us to the Officers' Club for Sunday brunch. Cruise-ship elegant, the Officers' Club was part of Columbia that we couldn't have experienced without Betty. It was something I had never wanted to experience and never expected to appreciate.

Betty transformed herself at Riverbanks. While she was helping to plant a bold, new garden, she opened new horizons for a crowd of young people, sharing the world where she'd spent her life — the Fort Jackson world of Columbia.

At 70 Betty had driven out of her orderly, organized military world, parked in an isolated lot, and walked into a metal-sided warehouse reverberating with loud Grateful Dead vibes and the vitality of a long-haired crew. She found a much-needed belonging as we built the Garden. Of course, what she also did was bring belonging to us, too.

It was eye-opening for me. I had never wanted to belong to the military world. But Betty was proud of that world and wanted me to understand a bit of it. She knew just the right parts to share with me — the parts that would help heal me into more acceptance of myself and others. There was a sweet irony in it all, of course.

11: Judging Pearl Fryar's Topiary Garden

Porter — once a volunteer but now the Garden's part-time plant records guy — took me aside one day to offer some advice. "You and I should explore the state together," he said. "There is a big horticultural history here in South Carolina, and I don't mean the grand camellia gardens and plantation gardens."

Porter grew up on the wrong side of the tracks. He wanted to take me to working-class gardens, where country gardeners did what they loved without rules or plant societies. He always said, "You don't know what you don't know. That research plant you're looking for may be out in some backwoods garden." Porter didn't push, but I knew he liked the research plant idea. So on Saturday mornings, we started doing little backroad field trips, mostly set up by Porter.

But one day I planned a trip with an ulterior motive. I told Porter we were going to a high school way out in the Pee Dee region of South Carolina to see a horticulture teacher and his greenhouses. What I didn't tell Porter was that I had met and been cruised by that horticulture teacher. His name was Jason, and he was a beefy, salt-and-pepper-bearded guy in a studly baseball coach sort of way.

Jason had been kind of drunk when we met at a happy hour for landscaper guys. He grabbed both my hands and leaned in like he was going to whisper but whispered slowly and loudly: "Come see me! I have great plants!' He had a sexy, country boy slur exaggerated by beers and a pleading sincerity. He stretched syllables about as far as anyone could and said, "Saturday, nine in the morning? All right? You will?" He started to grin. "At the high school back gate, you'll see the greenhouse. I can't wait."

At nine on the dot Porter and I pulled up to a locked gate and an empty greenhouse. We drove around town. Forty-five minutes later, still nothing but my deflated ego.

Porter knew I was pouting. We'd never talked about the gay thing. He was a teacher, a Baptist, and a Gamecock football fan. Some things you just don't need to tell a man like that.

We spent the morning in Kalmia Gardens. I kept my eyes open for research plants but no luck. On the way back, Porter said, "There's the exit where that topiary guy lives."

I'd heard about him and told Porter. "I'm not into that. All that control. I like plants set free, doing what they want to do. You know what I mean." A few people had mentioned this man to me. His name was Pearl Fryar, a self-taught topiary guy, a Black man, a factory worker who lived way out. Topiary conjured images of suburbia with sheared bushes and nothing more. But a museum friend told me, "You have to see his topiary. He works full time and does nothing else but his garden. You'll love him, and he deserves attention from the garden world. Professionals and garden clubs turn their noses up at him."

We were already all the way out here, so I decided to give in to Porter and took that exit ramp. No expectations other than that this was going to be a waste of time.

I parked the zebra van in front of a multi-colored brick ranch house. Secretly I hoped we hadn't been spotted, so we could just back out and find lunch.

No such luck, though, as a basketball player of a man quickly bounded up, grinning, with arms outstretched, and words tumbling out like bubbles from a bubble machine. "You're from the zoo? The Columbia Zoo? Fielding told me about you! Boy, I can't believe you're here."

Calling our mutual friend, Felder Rushing, "Fielding" didn't sit very well with me. Does this Pearl guy not really know who Felder is? Felder, a sort of hippy, redneck horticulturist, NPR radio show host and famous author, had done more to promote Pearl than anyone.

"Come on and see my garden!" He continued. "It's nothing like what y'all do at the zoo. I just pick stuff up from the trash pile outside of a local nursery."

Lurking ahead loomed dozens of multi-armed creatures. They were grazing, dancing, peaking out, and worshiping the sun. Little spider topiaries and elephantine creatures lazed on an endless, perfectly flat, green lawn — a zoo of sorts in its own right.

Pearl Fryar was over six feet of lean, chocolate muscle in jeans. He had a bit of gray and a hundred-megawatt smile. In his enthusiasm, he reached out and hugged me. He engulfed me. It was like being hugged by one of the crazy green creatures in front of me.

Pearl pulled me in. He focused on visions I couldn't see, and he talked about them like they were right there, plain as day.

"I just pick up a cast-off, and I know there's a beautiful plant in there. I can see it. Redeem it." With arms waving, he painted a picture. "It'll go like this, and then swirl over there. If I save this little twig, it'll become a loop one day, like a big hug. It'll be like it's reaching out to hug you!" He held two yaupon holly twigs, but he saw two hearts intertwined.

His voice was sonorous even out in this open field of creatures and cotton. His dialect and mispronunciations were lovable. He wanted us to sit in the "gra-zee-bo." Once there, Pearl Fryar launched into a monologue he'd been waiting to get out.

"I know all these children out there hear 'no' too much. They need someone to tell them, 'Yes! You can do that!'"

He leaned in and looked into my eyes. "I can say to them, 'Look at me! Who'd have ever thought I could make this beautiful? I may never get Yard of the Month from the people who give that out, but look at this! Believe it. You can do anything.'"

While he spoke, the Uncles in my head joined in: "We were just like those cast-off bushes! Malformed. Problems. Predators. That's what they said. Look at us now. Fabulous. That powerful sexy man, that misfit, made all this beauty. You remember that the ones they call problems might be exactly the guys you've been praying to meet."

———

My mind drifted while Pearl went on with his stories.

Recently, I had met this guy named Bob. A few acquaintances around town warned me not to accept a dinner invitation to his house. He had just left his wife and had been kicked out of society. They said he had a new young boyfriend, and he just wanted to do me, too. I decided then and there, listening to Pearl and the Uncles talk about doing things their own way, to ignore the folks who gossiped and to look for friends on my own terms.

Pearl kept right on talking.

"Farmer, you know they say you cannot grow a fir tree in this part of the state? Somebody from Clemson came here and told me. We were standing right here in front of this fir tree, and he told me I couldn't grow one." Though pruned up like a Dr. Seuss doll, this fir tree seemed perfectly healthy. Pearl reemphasized, "He said a fir tree won't grow in the Pee Dee!"

Proclamations annoy me. Pearl's story about a proclamation from an educated professional, standing in front of a growing fir tree, made me feel like we were on the same team. I finally had my eyes opened for me. Now, I saw Pearl the artist and his sinuous, strong, directed, flexing creatures. I heard his message from the outsiders club. No bushes here. This is all Pearl's passion.

While my mind processed it all, Pearl kept on: "Touch this. I like how the whole thing trembles when you touch just one little tip. Now Farmer, sit in the graz-ee-bo. I'll get some water. I'mma tell you the story. I wasn't supposed to be like this. There was this garden club that put out a Yard-of-the-Month sign around here. I worked and worked on my yard, but they'd never give me Yard of the Month. I knew it didn't have anything to do with pretty yards. Not one thing. A Black man, the man who brought the union to the can factory, would never ever get Yard of the Month. I decided to show them what I could do.

"Then the lady from the museum got it. A school brought a whole class on a field trip one day, and some of those kids got it. You know old Fielding, and you're here, and you get it. Can you believe it?"

When Pearl walked away to get those glasses of water, I said to Porter, "Do you think we could move a few of Pearl's plants?

Porter was visibly shocked and stammered, "Jenks, you just said you didn't like topiary! And you're always telling me to plant things that thrive. He's got a fir tree which shouldn't be growing in South Carolina anyway! And it's topiaried! On top of that, he doesn't use proper garden tools. He uses pantyhose and zip ties to hold things up! All that wire is going to strangle those plants. This isn't proper horticulture. Actually, it seems like a sure and slow death to me. You can't be thinking of a topiary collection? God Almighty! I mean, it's so different."

So different. Those words, used in this way, were old-school Southern talk. It's a polite expression meaning "so far out of the norm that it's not to be considered, not by people like us anyway." Different, in Southern parlance, is not a compliment. It hurt me that Porter was being part of that mindset. Sort of like the other critics, he was looking at the mechanics, not the message. Bible school and college classroom conventionality. It made me wonder even more about Porter. If I let myself speak freely around him, would he reject me? It reminded me that I needed to decide things for myself now.

Pearl Fryar bounded back into the gazebo and I said, "Pearl, will you come to Riverbanks Zoo and do a talk for us about all this? I'll get an audience of real gardeners together. They'll love it." I knew he had the charisma, but I didn't know if he had the desire.

"Farmer? What are you talking about? You are talking about me, standing up and speaking to garden club ladies, the same folks that won't give me Yard of the Month?"

I could see why Pearl might be hesitant, but he finally did agree to come to our quirky version of garden club talks.

———

Pearl would be perfect for the summer lecture series organized by the Center for Southern Studies at the University of South Carolina. The coordinator, Tibby Dozier Steedly, loved the idea. "We don't want to do fancy gardening talks," she stressed. "We want to invite weird and obsessed people who do crazy things with plants. Garden anthropology! We have some connections, but we need to round our list out with more plant people." Felder Rushing loved this entire idea. He drove over from Mississippi with his dog Rusty to kick off the classes and set the tone. Felder shared slides of little shacks with flower-filled porches as he told stories of plain people filling their yards with joyful petunias, gazing globes, and tire planters. He explained the different terms used in the evaluation of yard art. "Gaudy," he said, "means people may not like what you do, but they cut you some slack. Tacky, on the other hand, is when people think you don't know any better and say, "Bless your heart.'"

For the follow-up lecture, I drove Pearl to the Zoo. I knew he was nervous to do his first talk. Anyone would be. I didn't know how to ask if he was put off or nervous because of the makeup of our group — all White, urban, mostly university people. I saw Pearl as an equal, even a respected elder. How did he see me, a young White guy in charge of a lecture series and a brand-new botanical garden?

My small crew of gardeners was there but at this point we didn't have even one Black gardener. I grew up around Black gardeners and farmers who loved plants. Old folks. I wanted diversity on the crew. My efforts to pull together a racially diverse team had fallen flat. We had offered internships to Florida A&M, an historically Black college. I'd spoken to the Black garden club (there are two remaining all-Black garden clubs in the U.S. — in Philadelphia and in Columbia). It seemed young Black gardeners simply were not out there. No big surprise actually, given our state's abusive plantation history.

As a young and open gay man, I'd never really wanted to be on a landscape crew of butch, redneck, rough, straight guys. I partly understood how awkward it might feel for a young Black guy to be on our all White crew. I didn't know how to ask or change things. Maybe a man like Pearl could spark some changes one day.

The Zoo was empty at night. The attendees parked in staff spots and walked through the chain-link security gate, past the dark Flamingo Gift Shop. Siamang apes howled. Besides animals, we had the whole place to ourselves. People would drop by after work, hear and see some gardening info, and still have time to move on to their family or dinner plans.

Pearl did his first-ever public presentation in this humble setting. From up in the audiovisual booth I showed a few slides of his garden. Pearl stood with his back to the audience and pointed at things in his yard, talking to the screen. Then when he switched gears and turned around, he said "I just wanted to get that Yard-of-the-Month sign. I knew they'd never give it to me." He didn't say who they were, or why they'd never give him an award. "Now, look at me up here on a stage! Busloads of children coming to see my yard! Can you believe it?"

People fell in love. Pearl explained that he spoke through plants and he expressly wanted to get a message across to poor, country children like him who needed to be filled with hope and inspiration. He spoke to the children in all of us. The audience sat enrapt.

About 40 minutes in, I pulled two giant potted junipers onto the stage. He told us what he saw in each shrub. He pruned by hand a few minutes, releasing some inner beauty that only he could see. Then Pearl circled and said, "I see love in this bush. Here's how I start." He picked up his gas-powered hedge shears, cranked them, and went to work. It's fascinating to watch an artist at work. The audience wasn't so lucky this time because we had made a colossal miscalculation that ended the evening abruptly. In just a few minutes, no one could see anything. The auditorium filled up with blue smoke. People choked and ran out as I opened all the fire doors.

After things started to settle down, Pearl got a paper cup of punch. "Farmer, I swear, we should have known all that smoke would fill up the room. Can you believe it?"

Over the next 25 years, Pearl Fryer never once called me anything but Farmer. All through his career, he would call me up and say, "Farmer, I am going to Tokyo, Japan. Can you believe it?"

"Brazil! Farmer, can you believe it?"

"Farmer, I had 12 buses of children from local schools visit this week!"

"They're gonna make a movie, Farmer! I told them it had to be free for all of our local schools to watch."

"Farmer, that lady you sent put a tip in my box. A $5,000 tip! Can you believe it? "Man! Can you believe it?"

12: Seeking the Core Collection

One of my biggest tasks now was to define a plant that would represent Riverbanks and, therefore, Columbia.

It was my job to find this plant, then convince the world that it was worthy of being thrust into the limelight. This decision would affect my professional reputation here, back in Seattle, and everywhere in between. This plant would last for decades as Riverbank's core collection. It would set down roots and spread in the hearts of gardeners, acclaimed as a must-have among those with limited space as well as those with vast domains. It would live on for decades after me and would be the focus of long-term research and reputation.

As word about my search got out into the gardening community, I was flooded with invitations to see what others had planted and loved. Everyone wanted their plant to be the plant. John Windham, the most outgoing man of Columbia's most famous throuple, laid it on thick. "You must come and see our plants. We've brought home seeds from camping trips in Nepal, ashrams in India, and safaris in the Congo. I'll feed you, too."

John had given extravagant donations of plants and money to the Garden. He'd pull right up to the greenhouse doors with opera blaring and plants tumbling out of his minivan. A gregarious restaurateur, John was sort of a celeb sponsor on the art scene. His two long-time lovers were more reserved but equally engaged in life. The three men — John, Dr. Alfred Burnside, and Bill — had been together for decades. They established what became a pioneering AIDS research center that brought sick, confused, and often hopeless people from across the South to Columbia.

Before that, John ran Le Petit Château, Columbia's only restaurant to be featured in the gourmet magazine Saveur. It was not a place I could afford, so when handsome, enthusiastic John told me that he'd feed me as part of his garden invitation, I went.

Gin and tonics served in the sprawling kitchen made the visit cozy and familiar. That all changed, however, once I caught a glimpse of the dining room with its grand piano along with a table set with silver and crystal. That scene put me on edge and out of my comfort zone.

With a fresh gin and tonic in hand, we set off through 13 acres of a garden on the verge of returning to wilderness. They had decided years ago to release the garden from strict pruning, from conventional camellia cultivation. They enjoyed watching the garden figure out what it wanted to become.

A canopy of camellias dropped pastel petals on the path. A web of wisteria vines, thick as a thigh, made me want to climb. Sasanqua roots pried up the crumbled brick steps of a caved-in greenhouse from the 1930s garden, which had been laid out by a roving English horticulturist. Years of self-determination had overtaken and overgrown the southern imitation of British formality.

As we walked on, we found ourselves wandering through a reimagined Pangea — a Carolina Sandhills Asian jungle. Although chaotic and wild, the entire original collection was still tagged, numbered, and curated.

"Daddy started this collection in the '30s, just after he started the town of Arcadia Lakes" Dr. Burnside said. "He and his friends had a rich social and horticultural history tied to camellias." Dr. Burnside was launching into what I recognized as a sort of nomination speech. He wanted camellias to be our collection plant.

"Most of those old guys are dead now," Dr. Burnside continued, "but his good friend, Dr. Auld, wants to donate his entire camellia collection. He's been hunting for an interested young man for years. He's got typed lists, notebooks with dates, photos, prize trophies, and ribbons. You know in Daddy's generation those men were serious about their camellias. He wants to pass that down. I gave him your number. A camellia collection is essential to a Southern garden."

———

Everyone in town knew my job was to define the long-term goals and core plant collections for the botanical garden. Everyone had an agenda. I'd heard these speeches and pitches over and over at meetings, happy hours and lunches.

Via an embossed note card, I was asked to "Join the Iris Society ladies for lunch at AJ's. We'd like to talk to you about reticulatas!" I showed up in my work cargo shorts. The hostess kindly said, "I can seat you behind the palms." I added to her sentence in my head, "…where people won't see your inappropriate clothing."

"Meet me for Sunday dinner at Lizard's Thicket," said the Azalea Garden Club president. "I'll bring my granddaughter!"

"You need a bonsai collection. I have a Japanese garden, right here in Hampton Hills. Come to my moon-watching party!"

Most of the invitations came from Columbia's elite. I wasn't part of this society, but I had generational connections, and they wanted to use those connections to draw me in. They'd ask things like, "Your great uncle was the horticulturist at the State House, wasn't he? Are you related to Dr. Farmer of the Sanatorium? My father knew him through the Camellia Society."

I was related. I was the black sheep.

All these plants had strong and important ties to local history, especially the history of organized, social, wealthy, White horticulture. Any one of the plants pitched would have been acceptable. However, Jim, Melodie, all the gardeners, and I wanted to shake things up a bit. Even much of the administration was on board. We all wanted to connect regular people to plants, and none of these elite society "invitation" plants would serve our goal.

––––––

At the heart of many older museums and botanical gardens many core collections (plants or otherwise) are inherited. That collection may not be flashy, but it's the center. It gets attention from staff and outside professionals who do research and share intimate details, connections, history, photographs, and notes on items in the collection. Often this core collection is defined by the elite of town. The famed Barnes Museum in Philadelphia, for example, does have gardens established by Mrs. Barnes but her husband's idiosyncratic displays of impressionist paintings make up the core collection.

At Riverbanks we had an opportunity to say something bold and innovative. Lots of new gardens were redefining collections in modern ways. We were on board with that but respected one very important old way of doing things — building plant collections based on botanical classification. Jim recognized that one core collection plant would serve this tradition while also focusing and guiding not only us but also future staff. We wanted a single genus core collection.

We wanted our core collection plant to be one not yet explored in southern horticulture. It needed to be well adapted to our climate and soil and, if not native, related to natives. It needed to be easy for regular backyard gardeners to fall in love with and for them to fit it into modern landscapes. It needed to grow without intense chemicals or specialized care. Our plant definitely needed to turn heads and grab attention — the first step to pulling folks in, making them exclaim in wonder, and building bridges with all sorts of visitors.

The potential camellia donor, Dr. Auld, didn't call. He showed up unannounced and greeted me warmly. I like old guys, especially old guys with a plant passion. I knew this man had a lifelong passion that he was trying to pass on to a young man. His creased khakis and thin white Oxford shirt let me know he was in relaxation mode. In a way, I loved that these guys gardened and relaxed in clothes their wives bought at Belks and their housekeepers ironed with starch. His driver (also his gardener) was a gray-bearded Black man in a thin blue jumpsuit. He groaned as he got out of the driver's side of an overburdened pickup.

"Let's go through the list, and my man will get them all unloaded. You got that. Rosey?"

Now I groaned. I'd been around this sort of relationship early in life and had a concept that might have been a stereotype but often turned out to be true. An older White man employs a Black man to carry out projects and whims but pays him barely enough to live. It wasn't only the economics of it that grated on me, but it was that the White man seemed to believe the pretense that they were buddies engaged in mutual hobbies. This relationship was rooted in the history of plantations.

I hoped "his man" Rosey was named for President Roosevelt, not a collection of roses that might be coming along with Dr. Auld's camellias.

Camellia gentlemen grew these plants for single flowers only, which meant they pruned them severely, creating tortured trunks. Each fall, Dr. Auld or "his man" would meticulously strip the gnarly trucks of all but two or three buds. Then they'd carefully aim an eyedropper filled with chilled gibberellic acid right at the base of the remaining buds. The acid caused early flowering and gigantification. The goal was to try to force the gnarled trunk to produce one obscenely huge flower. That flower, scheduled and manipulated to open on the morning of the big camellia show, would be plucked, coddled, transported in a special case, and displayed at the show. It was about beauty, but it seemed to me to be even more about one-upmanship. Judges picked a winner, whose name would be engraved onto an antique silver platter, the Seibels Award. For bragging rights, the winner kept the platter for a year. Competitive gardening happens all over the world. It's not for me.

As Rosey unloaded plants, Dr. Auld pulled out a blue ribbon and photo sheet of crimson red, double, frilly camellia flowers. "This one is named in honor of Dr. Burnside. Old Dr. Burnside. Not the one you know. That one let his Daddy's camellias go to rack and ruin."

He sighed, silently pitying the vagrancy of the younger generation. I straightened my t-shirt, put my hands in the pockets of my unironed cargo shorts and tried to look like I felt his pain as he continued.

"The day we got this award, we were proud as a peacock. The day we won a blue ribbon, weren't we, Rosey? Yessiree Bob, we showed 'em who had the goods! And who won the silver platter that year? Put that down and show him the picture of the silver Seibles Award platter, Rosey."

I excused myself and called Jim. "Come help me. I cannot do this. I'm 100 percent sure we do not want these freak plants. If I take these things I'll be committing lots of time to plants that will just get thrown away, and I'll be lying."

Jim essentially told me to buck up. "Today, your job is to make this donor happy. Listen to me good. Smile. Call him sir. Ask him if he has any extra gibberellic acid. For the next hour, put your core collection aside and make this donor happy. I don't care if you have to commit to a date with his granddaughter. Do it. Try just once to fit in."

The Uncles sighed and ruffled my hair. "We went on a lot of dates with prom queens. You can do this."

For a second, I thought the Uncles were going to leave me with that encouragement, but one of them tried to distract me with a sordid camellia story:

"One gray winter day, I joined the Men's Garden Club of Jacksonville for a tour of the camellia garden. It's on the St. John's river, and from across the garden, a young, lonely sailor in dress blues attracted my attention. I broke away from the tour. It's easy among the camellia bushes. I wandered over just to ask him for a light and before I knew it..."

The Garden ended up accessioning all those camellias. A few made their way into hedge rows. Dr. Auld's awards and papers were preserved, but most of the camellias, like tired stories, needed to slowly fade away.

After that episode Jim was ready to settle the core collection question. "It's time to start the Museum Assessment Grant," he said. "Jenks, you've read it all, and answered the grant questions. Now you make me and Melodie answer all the questions, too. We control this. Donors do not. Push the limits, but be real with your answers. You know Riverbanks will never be an endowed research garden. Our pick must be easy to keep and manage, even as the staff changes. I've already asked the directors from Strybing Arboretum, San Francisco, and Chicago Botanic to come for a weekend to hear out and evaluate our decisions."

Designed to guide institutions, the American Association of Museums' grant program laid out a framework for diving deep, honing, winnowing, and making curators be realistic in assessment of what could actually happen given an organization's limits.

I knew the process. I'd been on the grant program's review committee for other gardens. This grant provided small funds to bring in professionals to explore core collection issues and have policies professionally written. It stimulated introspection and forced groups to find common answers. Jim liked the process of this, but he also needed the validation that would come at the end of the grant. At that point, we'd present our proposal to three botanical garden directors and three local professionals.

———

We scheduled time to debate different plants that I would nominate. By now we'd hired a part-time database manager, my old friend and volunteer, Porter. He was part of our upstairs attic office crew now, so while he worked quietly at his terminal, Jim, Melodie, and I listed pros and cons of various plants. Porter was generally quiet, doing research and entry while we talked. Sometimes, however, he told us Columbia stories that seemed like ancient history.

Born in 1933, Porter grew up in a textile mill village complete with a company store, community school, a gym with an indoor pool, and a giant shower room. Like many mill people, he grew up without indoor plumbing. That meant that Porter, his daddy, and brother went with the other men to the shower house a few times a week. Most of his friends ended up going to work in the mill, marrying early, and living in the village.

Generations of mill families living and working in the village gave it the stability of a closed, tight-knit community. One of my great-grandmothers lived and worked there, too. Even into the 1980s, West Columbia had a rough reputation among many downtown Columbians as being the wrong side of the river.

Porter's parents wanted more for him. They sent him to events and programs across the river, in the city. The more he saw there, the more he felt the limits of the mill life. He wanted to understand history, science, and the world. He also realized the world saw him and mill folks as limited. They called him "lint head," a pejorative term for the working class people who left work haggard and covered with lint from the textile mill.

Porter learned early to fit in, to stay quiet, to choose his words and timing. A master of quiet smiles, he deflected conversation with non-committal colloquialism, and patience. He didn't interrupt or join in our debates. He absorbed it all. I came to realize he had formulated his own agenda, his own proposal for a core collection.

Sometimes after Jim and Melodie had left the office, I'd ask what Porter thought of the conversation. He'd hold up a hand, with a chunky gold pinky ring and say, "Far be it from me to comment on what y'all have gone to college to study." Then he'd proceed to comment like some old hen.

But it was on our drives in the truck that Porter would open up. He drove me around the rough parts of town. Just minutes from the Garden's new gates was an area of former mill houses, two-story duplexes with tiny, plantless yards right beside the railroad tracks.

On one particular drive we stopped at a crumbling gym to poke around its once-roofed pool facility. From the deep end of the pool a bone-white trunk of trumpet creeper climbed the pool wall and up the remains of the high dive, spilling out huge scarlet flowers against the blue sky.

"Could vines be our collection?" I wondered out loud. "You know, Porter, in South Carolina, we have the second highest concentration of vines in the world? Second only to the Amazon."

Porter wasn't into it today. He seemed hell-bent on distracting me with stories of growing up in the mill village. "We came on Saturdays for swim lessons and a real bath," he said. "A massive locker room, showers, an afternoon of naked men. I guess it was the same anywhere, but lots of men and older boys bullied the younger ones like me. One was a low-down dog. Red-headed and with red hair all over his body just like a dog. Mean. If he was there, I'd skip my shower. He was the kind of man that would make a boy run away. Or worse."

Later Porter took me to meet a thin, worn man who grew angel trumpets outside a rickety Heyward Street mill house duplex. The railroad tracks were just a few feet from his back porch. He had gardened in the right of way. Porter introduced him to me. "This is Red. He has more types of angel trumpet than anybody and advertises in Market Bulletins in every Southern state."

Red proceeded to pick out some of the unusual angel trumpet plants that he thought the Garden should grow and wouldn't take a dime for them.

In the truck, Porter said, "Remember how I told you about that red-haired man? That dog? Well, that was Red's daddy. Red ran away before high school. Jumped on a train to Florida. Came back when his daddy died. I guess he found angel trumpets down there." I could hear in Porter's words his deep pride in the resilience of these mill people.

These poor people challenged me. I'd grown up on a farm with Daddy, who worked in a factory, but we had education and exposure to a broader world. We had a history of joyful storytellers, band leaders, and folks who had wanted us children to develop a broad worldview. In the mill village, I saw generational poverty and insular, conservative, religious people. I saw hopelessness. The mills were closing. One mill had been turned into a museum, its gymnasium was transformed into an art gallery. Another mill was eventually turned into condos.

I met Porter's gardening mill friends, but I was judgmental. I discounted their simple gardening around porches and clotheslines, and veggie gardens next to railroad tracks. I also discounted their common plants like angel trumpets, hibiscus, daylilies, crinum, and canna. All these plants are so easy to grow. The mill people and their plants didn't excite me.

I wanted the perfect plant, the one that my peers would think was a brilliant discovery, the one that met all of our goals, the one that would turn the head of any passerby. All these old plants in the gardens of the elite or the gardens of the mill just weren't cool enough for me.

Porter gently kicked me off my horticultural high horse.

'You know all these pass-along plants fit the bill," he said. "They are heat-tolerant. They have flowers so big that you think they're tacky. Regular people love them, and that means people have stories about them. That's what Riverbanks needs, right?"

Porter, the historian, teacher, coach, and mentor knew how to guide a young mind to reframe a situation.

"You're right. Maybe one of the summer bulbs." I sighed, overwhelmed.

Porter also knew when to focus on the moment, when to distract and let thoughts percolate. "Red's trying to breed a red one. Says he'll name it after his daddy."

The seed was planted. Some long-dormant bulbs waiting underground were about to emerge.

13: Gardening with Blue Collar Bonsai

Untouched sandwiches lay on the break room table with unopened cans of soda and an unread State newspaper headlined "Olympic Bomb Stuns The World." This was our gathering spot, backstage for the garden staff. It should have been bustling at noon on this hot day, but it was empty.

Then someone yelled from outside, "Rainey's hurt!"

I saw Rainey through the glass. He was laid out on a bench, back arched up, shirt ripped open, skinny little chest sweaty, and blood on his face. His torso squirmed while someone held his head steady. His eyes were wide open. Jack was calm in the middle of it all and focused on Rainey's bloody face as he squeezed a perfect stream of clear liquid from a bottle. After he flushed the wound, he gave Rainey a tight squeeze on each shoulder and told everyone to head into the break room for lunch.

Later, as Jack and I sat in the office, I tried to talk through all that happened earlier for Jack. "Sometimes I feel like this is high school. This is sort of our locker room. You're the cool guy, the unflappable soccer team captain. I appreciate your dealing with that accident and keeping everybody calm. I probably would have let it turn into unneeded drama."

"That branch that jabbed into his cheek coulda' hit his eye. Coulda' been worse," he said.

It became obvious that Jack didn't need to talk through it. He was good. We went back to looking at our computers.

Every day Jack and I got here earlier than anyone else. Both of us needed quiet hours with just a lamp and a calendar to gather steam before our extroverted sides could wake up, which both of our jobs required. In that quiet time we were like brothers thinking before the house lights went on. This was a time of serenity and silent bonding.

Some mornings we'd walk through the greenhouse or nursery and just be with our plants. Jack's job was to bring plant dreams to life. This meant that he was always working toward something. And he was always nursing some tiny seedlings through the heat of August so they'd be ready for the cool October days they loved.

Melodie and I planned seasonal plantings for eight months down the road and new exhibits years ahead. Jack had the knack of taking our messy spec lists and our dreams of obscure plants and turning them into reality. He was the finder of materials needed and the planner of deeds to be done by deadlines a year away.

As Jack and I took our morning walks, anyone listening to us talk might have wondered about us and what we were up to. He'd say things like, "Jenks, the cardoon is germinating and will look great for October." And a little further on, he might point out and ponder with me. "Look at these tiny hairy leaves. I can't get Adlumia to do anything. It must need a warm-then-cold regimen, and even the fridge can't trick it."

Jack's ever-present calmness seemed to play well with my more erratic nature. But I was secretly envious of his calm. His self control. When the coffee kicked in, I got wound up and into the energy of the crew. We'd even go out for beers after work.

But Jack headed home. Not only was he married, but also his ever expanding bonsai collection needed water and care — especially on hot days. And Jack needed his bonsai.

———

We had talked a bit about having some bonsai specimens in the Garden, but I finally needed to put that idea to bed. "It doesn't fit, Jack. This is the South. Too hot. You have to water them too much. I don't really understand why you love bonsai. Why's a farm boy from Michigan into Japanese bonsai anyway?"

Jack looked at me, and in his ever-calm way, started to process all that was implied in my question. I knew Jack, and I knew it would be a while before he opened up about that part of his life.

One holiday morning with just the two of us working. Jack finally told me the story:

"When I was in the Army in Korea, most guys stayed on base, but I'd left a little farm in Michigan to see the world, not just the Army base. So I would often set out on my own. I couldn't read or speak Korean, but I realized the buses had a simple numbering system and ran straight uptown then came back downtown. So I got on the 23 bus heading in one direction. I'd count stops. Then I'd jump off the bus and wander around. To get back, I'd catch the 23 going the other way, count stops, jump off, and head back to base.

"I had two favorite stops. One was in a part of town called the Green Zone. Every shop was filled with plants, garden tools, cut flowers, shrubs, and forced bulbs. There was a bonsai shop, too. Even though I had never heard of bonsai before, I soon came to realize that being in that zone with that bonsai shop changed my energy. It changed how I felt."

Jack and I were exactly the same when it came to traveling. I was never one to sit around when I traveled either. I wanted to know the other stop he discovered that he liked so much.

"It was a street that had endless tiny restaurants," he continued. "I picked it randomly. The waitress pointed to a table. I sat. Then she came over, and at that moment we both knew. It was love at first sight," he said. "Her name was Jung."

Jack and Jung eventually moved to Michigan, near his family farm, where he enrolled in Michigan State to study horticulture. Working in the university's Beaumont Nursery, Jack learned that a research nursery or a public garden nursery was a totally different beast from a retail nursery. He learned specialty propagation and cared for special collections plants, each with unique water, soil, and fertilizer needs. He read professional journals, including The Public Garden, a publication of the American Association of Botanical Gardens and Arboreta.

"That was my first real place to start to build my collection of bonsai," Jack said. "But I didn't see bonsai as a career. I started looking for jobs in public gardens."

"Everyone in the profession in the US knew about Riverbanks' new garden. Jim Martin wrote about it. He lectured about it. At the same time, horticulture was taking off as a backyard hobby. And for many of us, Riverbanks' new endeavor seemed like a culmination of that. And all that was happening in a small southern town that nobody had ever heard of. It was a great story that was getting attention."

Jack smiled, "But I had heard of this little town since I'd been in boot camp at Fort Jackson. So I applied. Now, here I am. Back in Columbia but with bonsai."

"And a wife," I added.

Jack smiled with a nod.

I knew Jack would love to see us incorporate bonsai. He'd been active in the local bonsai society and even hosted the group in the Garden. But I resisted, "Jack, it just seems too intense for our climate. And it seems elitist."

He persisted. "But that is completely untrue. Bonsai was brought to this country with the bluest-collar, hardest-working guys ever — the soldiers who went to Japan for reconstruction after World War II. It came to the U.S. with the same kind of guys who've retired all around Fort Jackson."

This kind of blew me away, "Come on, Jack. How do army guys get credit for bringing an ancient Japanese gardening art form to this country?"

He had an answer ready. "From Eisenhower down through the ranks, there were organized classes to teach ground infantry to appreciate the culture and arts of Japan. There's a beautiful irony to the young grunts learning ancient, elegant traditions. Soldiers, many of whom were regular guys, brought home a passion for the ancient art of bonsai. Men like John Naka and Harry Hiaro promoted, shared, and encouraged others in the United States to find peace and pleasure in bonsai. I actually met them. They believed that if everyone cared for bonsai, the world would be a more peaceful place. They believed that bonsai could bridge cultures and history."

Jack's quick history lesson put a new light on bonsai. We did have a huge retired military population and many of our volunteers came from around the Fort. He was telling me exactly what we'd all thought, discussed early on when planning the Garden — that it would be a garden for real people, ordinary people, unlike the exalted but tired southern gardens of the past which were made for and by the elite.

This story helped me understand Jack. I assumed that he was born all calm and contemplative. That his ability to jump in and handle a crisis, like a gardener bleeding from near his eye, was innate. But I got it now; Jack worked for this. Some people do therapy or yoga. Jack did bonsai.

As for me, I started gardening with a ghost.

14: Living with a Ghost in a Bohemian Paradise

"Willie Freeland's house? You live there?"

When I told folks where I lived, people who'd grown up in Columbia knew of the place. Willie Freeland wrote a garden column for The State newspaper and made one of the first PBS garden shows, The Garden Spot, years before the more successful 1975 Victory Garden.

Willie the Digger tottered around, cardigan buttoned up, spewing Latin names, snipping prize ivy plants, and packing up their cuttings to send off to clients. When Willie went back into the ground himself, his place quickly went wild as spirits and vines took over.

At first, it was my Bat Cave — a secret place to garden, hide, and write. Just me.

But sometimes I sensed Willie around. My guess was that he needed to have a little more fun than he'd had in life, to let his hair down, and keep an eye on his plants.

In the back yard Christmas tree bamboo pushed up through deck holes. A thick and hairy ivy trunk, like a chimpanzee arm, came through the window holding a sort of topiary fist of greenery. Which I pruned. Just a little. I imagined that I could hear Willie's approval:

"It's proper that you left it growing in the window. It's mine after all. You realize it's Hedera 'Dragon Claw'. Spectacular, isn't it? One of my best sellers."

Being alone with the unseen Willie so much of the time, I began to appreciate our conversations. Ever the professor, Willie posthumously started teaching me about his collection of vines. These marvelous beings found their wild again after he died, weaving ground to sky, dirt to roof, and past to future. Not just ivy either. A dinosaur-sized Banksia rose seemed to cover the entire house with an avalanche of butter-yellow March flowers. Blood-spotted golden crossvine and silver lace vine ran thick in the pines. Massive vine trunks climbed up trees, where their shoots crept horizontal like rattlers, leapt out of the top, and raced across treetops toward Gills Creek.

The house had been abandoned for a decade before I moved in. Porter owned it. He got me power but no a/c and no heat. Life in an unheated house isn't so bad in the South. Lots of folks just close off most of the house in January and February, and use a small heater in the kitchen and bath. I slept in the dining room on a futon with a black-and-white photo of Willie at a typewriter by the big bay window. Looking at that photo one evening, I said aloud, "I'm taking over this spot now, Willie."

He cackled. "Where's your typewriter? Where's your mimeograph? Can't run an ivy nursery and can't write for the newspaper without those!"

Willie gazed suspiciously at the laptop.

Letters still came for Willie. "Dear Mr. Freeland, please send your current ivy list. Please find a SASE enclosed."

Some letters made my heart swell, so I'd write back, and break the sad news. Willie watched and edited. I told him, "I'm being respectful and demure, Willie. No worries. I know how you old guys hide in plain sight, sneak around in the camellia bushes on occasion, and expect us all to maintain your facade. I wouldn't repeat the things you say to me for all the tea in China. And you know that I know that I'd be the one looking like a crazy, old, reclusive queen if I ever told anyone that I lived with the ghost of a TV gardener."

In life Willie had been a church-going man, prim but gentle, and married. He was exactly the type of man that someone's brash and crazy aunt might have lassoed and dragged out of Plum Branch, South Carolina. He never complained about having been captured. He went through life bemused, resigned to his role, tending his plants.

This was a new world, though. My world, the 1990s. Vines and Willie could be liberated now. When I gardened, Wille watched from way up in the spindle tree while I sorted through his collection of old washing machine tub planters. He always laughed when I cussed at one of those tubs that had been totally rooted into the ground. Then he stood over by the empty pond and made popping sounds with his lips around his smoking pipe. It doesn't take a pipe smoker to get that pipe popping sounds are tantamount to a verbal reprimand. But I'm pretty sure I heard some giggles of delight, too.

While gardening late one afternoon, I heard giggles and looked up to see Willie, hands on his hips, and speaking in his best Truman Capote accent. "This was a proper garden. Respected. On TV. Look at you, though!," he popped his pipe. "You're working in my garden, in broad daylight, in your boxer shorts!" Willie was one of my few friends, noisy and maybe just a little cantankerous in a loving way. But in the back of my mind, I'd decided that I wanted to get some actual flesh-and-blood friends.

———

To help make this happen, I planned a Halloween party. I decorated the place and even made a huge inflatable snake, 100 feet long and 10 feet in girth. It was painted orangey brown and rust. I inflated it with a box fan and lit it up with internal Christmas lights. Its forked tongue stuck onto the Rosewood sidewalk; its puffed body arched over the roof of the house; and the blunt tail touched the back deck.

On the night of the party, that snake and my firepit glowed. My biological and very alive uncle sleazed in first, wearing full leather gear and accompanied by a nearly naked young man on a chain. My uncle was eerily quiet all night except to answer inquiries about his costume. But I knew it wasn't a costume. All he'd say was, "Do not pet the pup."

Madonna showed up next. This particular '80s trashy, Like-a-Virgin Madonna came right up to me and said, "Don't look so confused. You invited me. I have the invitation right here. Wanna see?"

"No need," I replied, thinking I would figure out who she was as the night progressed. The point of the party, after all, was to meet new and creative people. That goal had inspired me to hand out invitations penciled with Day of the Dead skulls and my address to random people. She was most likely one of those people.

Seeing all the thoughtful costumes and the creative people who wore them made me feel alive. I finally felt some hope that I would find a few interesting people hiding among this boring little town's legion of conformists.

After I had met Pearl Fryar, I realized something about myself. I'd been judging and condemning folks who, at first glance, were trying to fit into this conservative culture. I was excluding them without giving them a chance to show me their real selves.

Ever since I came to town I'd heard about this older guy named Bob. Plenty of folks warned me to keep my distance. They said he'd been a respectable, family man, banker type, all involved with music and groups at the city Cathedral and local non-profits. It all changed, though, once he met handsome and charismatic Eric. Eric was confident, a rule breaker, and half Bob's age. Educated but irreverent. It didn't take long before they had moved into a Victorian house surrounded by its own gardens and set up a sort of commune with a couple of other gay guys and two young women who wore boys' clothes.

I liked everything I saw. Especially Eric. He was bald, bearded, compact, and loved plants. Eric could have been my Huck Finn gardener love. We'd go for sunset walks in his garden and take a smoke. Occasionally, he'd join me on Saturday road trips.

Bob played a fatherly role in my life. He always looked like a banker or a lawyer, all suited up. For a while, I even suspected that he wanted to get me to wear some "proper clothes," the preppy uniform I had vowed forever to avoid. He even started picking out potential dates for me, but I figured that he knew only blue blazer preppy boys.

My Halloween party wasn't quite Bob's cup of tea, but he attended and brought other friends, too. Standing around the fire, Bob said, "We're gonna find your Huck Finn, your gardener-man boyfriend. He's in Columbia somewhere. He and Columbia need you to settle down here."

"Bob, there's no man for me here. It's not that I don't try. This morning, at work, a tree-truck driver with a shirt patch that said 'Buddy' delivered trees. He was a blond, compact guy with thick forearms, a crooked smile, and sharp blue eyes. Sexy."

Bob smiled as he let me finish my story.

"Buddy had been unloading magnolias from his truck with a forklift, but his eyes were on me the whole time. I know he was cruising me. I signed the invoice and told him to come to the Halloween party. He didn't say a word. Men are scared here. He was just some white-trash hot flash, as the old queens would say."

Bob laughed and I smirked.

I was wearing huge striped genie pants that I'd made, copied from a David Bowie poster. No shirt. A guy from the piercing crowd butted into the conversation and pinched my nipples. "We need to get you some jewelry. On the house. This would be great advertising."

Bob wandered off, and Madonna joined me by the fire. "I heard you talking to that old guy. Just so you know, you didn't scare me. And I can be a white trash hot flash all day long. But you're not really my type. I knew that when I was unloading the magnolia trees today." Madonna grinned and pulled up a skirt to point out hairy blond thighs and a bulge.

15: Touring a Handsome Journalist

B ob and Eric had a tradition of hosting Sunday night dinner at their house. In just a few weeks, I was a regular there. And Bob was a man on a mission for me, so he started to invite single guys to dinner on Sunday evening.

One night, he introduced me to one of his new guests. "Pat is a journalist. He writes "Talk About Town". It's a witty, daily, what's-happening-in-town column. Y'all talk."

I immediately noticed how pale he was. This guy never went outside. He probably wore ties. And pressed slacks. He probably had an iron to press his slacks. Ugh. That having been said, his sparkling blue eyes and curiously curly, auburn hair made an impression on me.

In the kitchen, I whispered to Bob. "He's the whitest guy I've ever seen. I bet he wears tighty whities. And I hate that newspaper."

As the dinner unfolded I tried to carry on conversation with Pat. But the best I could do centered on my failing multiple English classes. My inner critic wondered why in the hell I would tell a writer that. Obviously, a bad start. Oddly enough though, Pat seemed to enjoy my stories.

Pat called at work the next day. "Hey, that was fun last night at Bob and Eric's, but I'm calling about work. Could I come out, get a behind-the-scenes tour, maybe write about some of the odd things that happen on a garden construction site?"

When he arrived at the Garden, he wasn't wearing a tie. His shirt was pressed but with far more buttons unbuttoned than I'd have expected. In fact, in the sun, he was ruddy, windblown, and sexy in an Irish farmer sort of way. His thin fingers had a life of their own. Mesmerizing. He could talk, pen notes, and flip pages in a narrow notebook, all at the same time. He was a lefty, too.

"It'll just be a short happy paragraph," Pat said. "You know, new guy in town. And some fun interaction with the other gardeners. Can I meet the crew?"

We were still a fairly small crew, and Pat seemed to get along well with all of them, making people laugh while also asking pointed questions. He laughed easily, too, especially at plant stuff he didn't know. It was sort of like he used that as a way to get the crew to loosen up with him. He'd point out all the things he didn't know, enjoy watching the crew laugh at him, and then marvel at the stories it elicited from the crew.

Everyone talked about him later at break. They liked him. I didn't bother to tell Jim or anyone from the Zoo press department. It seemed innocent enough. Of course it didn't turn out that way.

16: Bonding Over an Escaped Convict

For a few weeks our team was able to walk from the Zoo to the Garden's construction site by balancing on a single but massive poured concrete girder. It was high, exciting, dangerous, and we were young, confident, and had balance. Our heads touched golden hickory leaves above while 20 feet below, kayakers glided over white water rapids through rocky shoals that connected the rich wooded hills of the Piedmont to the dry sandhills.

Admin and lawyers quickly ended that risky way to connect the Garden's world with the Zoo's world. The result was that our small crew ended up working alone and isolated from the late fall through winter. No phone lines. No computers. No backstage drama from the Zoo. Blissful in its own way, but it was time to fill out our small crew and make us feel less isolated. Of course, we also needed a larger garden crew to transform this muddy mess in time for the springtime opening day of the Garden.

When I brought all of this up with Jim, he made a flippant suggestion that riled me up, and I exploded, "The labor pick-up point on Millwood! You want me to load a few guys in the pickup bed every morning? Then drop them off in the afternoon. Those guys won't work. They are going to smell like liquor and sweat, nap in the port-o-let, and brag about the women they fucked last night. Only they'll be nastier than that. And if I'm honest about who I am, they'll call me a fag. It'll be a series of endless jeers. I've been there, Jim. So no."

My sound logic and truth-telling didn't seem to have much effect on Jim. I had to say something to convince him that this was an untenable idea. "But here's something else you need seriously to consider. I can lie. I can play straight and pass for it if I have to, Jim. You can't. They'll definitely make fun of you. Then I'll have to try to buddy up with the crew in order to get anything done. I'll have to head back into the closet and be complicit in what they say about you behind your back. You've got to see how horrible of an idea this is."

This bit of future-tripping with Jim seemed to do the trick. "You're right, Jenks. It's a bad plan. Try to find the crew you want. Just don't hold your breath."

But that night, some politically connected power players hatched up a plan that made the labor pick-up point idea look not so bad. Those power players wanted to use prison labor to round out our garden crew.

I argued against it the entire next day.

———

My complaints were all wasted breath because two days later, a solid black bus with blacked out windows pulled down the dirt construction road. That bus barely fit, breaking off white oak limbs along the way.

As it approached, I could see only its brooding front with four giant headlights. I felt like I was looking down the barrels of two double-barrel shotguns. The prison labor bus hissed to a halt.

I tried to make the best of it. Apparently, these were guys picked for this job because they worked well on a nearby prison farm. As I addressed them, two armed guards in stiff polyester uniforms cut me off and barked orders at me. "You can tell them what to do for the job only. Anything else, like bathroom or rest breaks, you have to go through us."

"Will do. Can we chat with them while we work?" I asked.

"Inventory all your tools as you hand them out."

I started handing out manure forks, with wide curved tines. "Hell no, son! They cannot use that pitchfork!"

I don't mind being called son, but this crewcut geezer brought bad energy to our happy woods. I was about to make a radio call to ask for an immediate conference with Jim when one of my new part-timers stepped in. "Let me talk to 'em," Tommy said in his Walterboro brogue. "You show the men what to do. I'll deal with the guards."

Tommy took over like a pro, addressing the guards as equals.

Tommy joined our team as a tool and equipment guy. In a previous life, he had worked his way through the prison system and recently retired. In his interview, he informed me: "Now, I still am an active hostage negotiator, so if there's ever a situation, I won't be here that day."

Sure enough, one morning I heard a news report about a prison riot in Ohio. A little later, I got a voice message from Tommy saying, "Hey Bo', I'll be gone until I get back."

He had agreed that this prison labor thing was a dumb idea. "Three hundred acres of endless woods, a massive river, and just downstream sit suburban homes where everyones gone off to work. What are they thinking?"

Scenes from the old movie, Cool Hand Luke, played in my head. By two o'clock, we were living that movie when one of the prisoners bolted. SUVs sped into our space. Sirens screamed. Muscle-bound, camouflaged troops swept the area. Bloodhounds sniffed around my huge compost pile and through our bushes then faded into the woods.

Another team of guards, also in camo, brought work to a halt and locked us all in the construction trailer. The bricklaying crew, a bunch of Brazilian guys who were constantly stoned, huddled in a corner.

Patrol cruisers of every sort combed the nearby neighborhood. Across the river in the Zoo, staff locked office doors, a field trip of school children were secured in the Flamingo Gift Shop, and visitors were herded into the Kenya Cafe. Helicopters swarmed overhead.

The local media descended, and the escape was all over the radio and television in no time. On cue at six o'clock, a local news anchor broadcast the unfolding story as officers pulled the runaway prisoner out of a carport that belonged to an empty-nester couple. The prisoner had folded himself up into a little cabinet on top of a stand-up freezer full of frozen okra and juice pops.

The next morning's paper, of course, had to report on the situation. The story wasn't on the front page, only the B section. A little column on the left. Above the fold: "Inmate Escaped at the Zoo!"

Pat had already been writing his story about the Garden crew when all this drama went down. It had been all over the TV news. What else would any responsible reporter do but report on it, right? Besides, he wrote it in a kind of tongue-in-cheek style. I smiled a little as I read it and saw that Pat had a lovely, dry wit and that we shared an appreciation of the absurd.

❦

17: Falling in Love on the Bamboo Deck

At daybreak the next morning, when I was usually alone, the Zoo's PR people showed up on my construction site. They called Jim and me to their van. Jim shook his head. They fumed. They ranted. "We manage the press. You garden. You cannot ever again talk to any member of the press or bring them onto this site without us present!"

"Oh boy," I thought. "Can I just get back to work, and y'all get back to your conformist offices?" It wasn't like I even knew press people. Or like anyone wanted the low-down stories on the Garden from me. I brushed it off until one of those press department people commanded, "And don't talk to that reporter Pat anymore!"

I went into the trailer to call Pat and ended up having to leave a message on his machine. "You won't believe this, but you got me in trouble. I'll tell you more later. Can we have a lunch date? Friday? I'm vegetarian, but the Basil Pot is too slow. I have only a short lunch break. Meet me at my house?"

Friday was one of those spectacular crisp days when the sun warms your skin, when you wear shorts and a sweater in the morning, but shed shirts by two p.m. I planned for us to eat on the deck. But the deck needed pruning. It had become the Angkor Wat of decks and half disappeared under determined vegetation. Fishing-pole bamboo canes coming up through the floor made the deck a maze, while cross vine provided a lacy curtain on one side. I carved out room for two chairs and a table. I snipped vines off my yellow ten speed, leaving it to give the impression that I had other interests besides plants.

Pat arrived. Amazed. "I drive by here every day. I never knew there was a house here."

We ate on the deck, and his amazement didn't fade.

"Purple potatoes? I've never had them. Did you grow them in the garden?"

"No, Pat, it's not potato season." That sort of ignorance on anyone else's part would have made me roll my eyes. But with him, it was charming.

He laughed incredulously when I opened a bottle of wine. "I thought we both had to go back to work."

Pat spoke authoritatively about his work and journalism. He told me about the tight relationships that form in the newsroom. He laughed easily. He somehow laughed, grinned, and said yes at the same time, especially in response to the stories I told him about living in this funky house.

We wandered around my small house. He picked up an old yellow newspaper off the desk. It was the same paper Pat wrote for, but this copy was 30 years old. His thin finger flipped and scanned one of Willie's old columns and he did a quick critique: "I like his Southernisms. Today, we'd say he was guilty of doing something journalists call 'burying the lede.' I think he just wrote like he talked. Southerners can be slow to get to the point."

We went back to the deck to finish the wine.

"That's what y'all Midwesterners think," I thought as I watched Pat's thick auburn chest hair peep out of a pressed button-down shirt. I can be pretty quick when I see something I want.

Auburn tangles turned into waves disappearing under a belt. There's only one good thing about slacks: they unzip easily.

Tiny, red dots popped up on Pat's back a little while later. With skin as white as copy paper, the vines above us cast distinct shadows connecting those dots. I traced the map on his back. He blushed. "I've never had mosquito bites there before."

After Pat had left, Willie popped in. He loved that they'd written for the same newspaper. He implied that I needed someone like Pat to up my reading skills. Willie even got all literary, quoting Truman Capote: "A really beautiful redhead is rarer than a flawless, forty-carat, pigeon-blood ruby — or even a flawed one, for that matter."

The quote went way over my head. I rolled my eyes and quipped, "Don't get excited, Willie. It was just one time."

Willie cackled.

18: Settling in with Crew and Friends

Despite having been told we couldn't afford creative, dedicated folks, my plan was a success. The new crew meshed quickly with the existing staff. They respected Jim, and they all loved Melodie, who brought great plants, gossip, and stories from behind the scenes at the Zoo.

Some of the people we added included a disillusioned truck driver, a Nordic lesbian sick of the sexism in waitressing, a Brazilian artist, and a hair stylist who thought he might turn gardener. They were all in some sort of transition, searching, and all excited to be part of planting something that would live beyond us.

They got how this was a chance to do something that would become a part of the fabric of the city forever. They bought in as I explained what the mission and creativity of a botanical garden should be. They were all good with working a few months for low pay with the promise of opportunity for personal satisfaction.

We did more than shovel compost. We got to know each other, and we shared physical challenges while we shared a vision. We worked long days together in the chill of cold drizzling rain and eventually in the warmth of spring glory. We traded leftovers and takeout food on a picnic table or in our breakroom. After work, we hung out together. All misfits, we became like a family, overlooking idiosyncrasies, accepting faults, and helping each other with our personal insecurities. It was a powerful prescription for quick and lasting bonds to develop.

Pat joined us during our after-work gatherings more and more frequently. He'd come late. He'd stay late. And after the crew left, he'd spend the night.

One night, after a little gathering, Pat and I ate some special mushrooms and decided to explore the garden. For some reason, the mushrooms led us to a charming chimpanzee who seemed to live in our bamboo grove, though we had never met him before. Back in the house, Pat discovered a man dressed up in a chicken suit, who seemed to live happily under the futon.

Many Joan Baez albums later, when it was time to go to bed, we couldn't sleep inside on top of our chicken-man friend, so we pulled the futon onto the back deck and zoned out under the stars.

We slept late into the morning and woke up to find two baskets of breakfast at our feet. One had little pastel plastic eggs decorating it. We'd totally forgotten that it was Easter, but at least two thoughtful people had played the Easter bunny and visited us as we slept naked on the deck. At least we had had a quilt over us.

Pat was confused as he got up to make the coffee. I was curious what was in the baskets. As I lifted a cloth sort of Tibetan prayer flag from the top of the more rustic basket, I found an array of crunchy-topped muffins.

I walked into the kitchen with the baskets. I showed off the rustic basket first. "My crew leader. My right-hand woman. Remember the one I call GOGO? Not to her face, of course. She used to be a baker, and this basket of muffins has to be from her."

I imagined the maniacal laughs and ribbing I'd get Monday morning from GOGO.

This other basket was low, tightly woven. It held shiny apples, firm yellow bananas, and biscuits tidily wrapped in Saran wrap. "This basket has to be from my volunteer Betty. I'm sure she's never seen two naked men spooning. She is very proper and sports a blue-ish perm. You know what? She'll love you."

I smiled at the thought of the two of them meeting.

Being observed sleeping naked on the deck with my new boyfriend didn't elicit the reaction I had dreaded. Only full-body joy. Neither of the ladies who'd done such a sweet thing ever said anything more than "We're so happy y'all found each other."

We were family now.

🌱

19: The Boss Come Out in an English Way

Even covered with gravel, scaffolding, and backhoes, the Garden construction site started to reveal itself as a Southern version of an English walled garden. Even though we'd agreed to change the plant pallet, Jim continued clinging to the influence of the English-garden style. It was pervasive in the garden media of the '90s. He loved ancient history combined with the modern English styles of it all. But it made no sense in our climate, and it frustrated me.

He knew we had to find a better way, using climate-appropriate plants with climate-appropriate styles. He just had a tough time letting go and continued to micromanage. The rest of us needed him to leave for a while and give us some space, so we could put the kibosh on the English-garden pretensions.

On a rainy Monday morning with garden work stopped, Jim, Melodie, and I met in our attic hideaway office. It was like old times. Melodie picked out CDs, Jim made hot tea, and I made coffee. Jim was full of energy. He'd just returned from a conference and launched into a story that began, "You won't believe the weekend I had!"

I thought, "Finally! He went to Raleigh, got laid good and hard, and he's seen the light. We're gonna all laugh and cringe as he tells this head-over-heels, love-and-lust story."

But nothing so fun as that.

"I met Rosemary Verey, Sir Christopher Lloyd, and Penelope Hobhouse at the garden symposium. They're garden royalty and they asked me to visit them in England and promised to show me how they do things. Off-season, when they're not overwhelmed with tourists. This will be my insider's trip. This time just me and some real gardeners. I'm not leading, teaching, or tucking in the society ladies."

This trip to England was going to be Jim's dream come true. He'd finally built personal relationships with the Who's Who of English gardening. The stars had aligned in one single weekend while at a garden symposium held in a faux English village in North Carolina. And it had left him breathless.

I tried to envision how this had all come out during the weekend symposium. With gregarious Jim it wasn't difficult to imagine as he talked about how after a day of lectures, he had found the cozy hotel bar where all the British gardener speakers retreated from the heat and the crowd. They all laughed as J.C. Raulston shyly shared a story of the absurdity of the South. J.C., probably desperately wanting diversion, was thrilled to see Jim sitting alone with a bottle of white wine.

Charming Jim joined the crowd of older speakers, thrilling them with his stories of zebras rutting off zelkova bark, tortoises eating giant allium, and gardeners weeding among busloads of kindergarteners. Jim could tell a story about the humilities of gardening in a zoo with exaggerated and engaging indignation.

I could hear his excited, almost shrill voice, as he entertained the British elders with his anecdotes. He probably said things like, "Y'all talk about all those little bugs and bunnies and cute pests, right? But have you ever had a sea lion in your border? I planted the most beautiful combination of Indo Spires salvia with a bit of pink cleome seeded in. It was a perfect combination set under the rustling sabal palms in a June breeze. Then one morning, right at dawn, I went to deadhead only to find sea lions rolling about in my salvia bed! Have you ever, ever tried to shoo a sea lion? With only the stems of a Sabal palm? They bend, you know. Palm fronds bend against a sea lion's rubbery skin."

Soon enough, Jim had booked his flights. We all wanted to say: "Cheerio, Jim. We'll fix things while you're gone."

———

A few weeks later, we gathered in our attic office before dawn as Jim made his entrance. The air filled with stories of charming old ladies, knighted men, and the authors of glossy English garden coffee table books inviting Jim to drink sherry in their greenhouses. Another story began with Rosemary Verey making him a cup of tea in the kitchen. "It was a dream!" Jim gushed. "I was ready to bond and gossip with her at first sight! I had a tape recorder. But before she had said a word, she fell asleep. Sitting across from her at the kitchen table, what was I supposed to do? I looked out the window at the garden, watching darkness fall, and waited for her to wake up!"

I thought,"Oh, Jim, this was your dream? Seriously? You went to England and didn't use your earnest, blond American charms to get laid?"

Jim gave me a sideways glance as if he had read my thoughts.

"One night I stayed in this tiny village. We'd been on a conservation walk in the moor when a freezing rain whipped up. I didn't want to do anything but shower and crawl in bed. But later, it cleared up and turned out to be a lovely night. I even went out for a late walk. As I strolled past closed shops, I happened to look up to a second-floor window and saw cozy light and silhouettes. So I climbed up some creaky stairs and joined a pub full of working guys having a pint.

"It was just synchronicity. There wasn't a sign or a flag or any indication. But I knew when my foot had cleared the top step that this was the gay pub. It was so normal. I wanted that. Back home you had to go to a gay bar. Back home the bars were so gay. And you know, all private. You have to join just to get a glass of chardonnay! It's too much. Such a process, a lifestyle, a definition. These guys were just having a beer. I was stunned and delighted to find them, just to walk in on this. I stayed and talked for hours."

I had to ask. "Well? Did you get it on with some sheep farmer behind the dartboards, or in the loo, or anywhere dark and dank?"

He huffed at my crudeness. "I'm serious. It was real. This was a moment."

That moment at the pub did have an effect on Jim. It actually changed him. He was more comfortable with himself. Formerly tight-lipped and compartmentalized, Jim now planned to go to the Marches on Washington and to the Black Party in New York. At work, over the next several weeks, he relaxed and let me run things more and more.

He brought this new confidence to work in other ways, too. Besides speaking at the Junior League and the Fort Officer's Club, Jim added the South Carolina Gay and Lesbian Business Guild to his roster. He arranged for the entire crew to do a fabulous display of flowers at some black-tie, gay fundraiser. Jim was finally being himself.

One night over beers, I asked him about Ryan Gainey, the notorious South Carolina rebel turned Atlanta garden designer. "Do you still want that Ryan sort of thing? Fabulous greenhouse, showplace of a garden, the reputation?" My question was intended to be about work, about garden style. Jim's mind was elsewhere.

"Ryan melded the ancient English garden vibe with Southern exuberance," he said. "I could never be that fabulous. Back when I was gay-away, in Atlanta, or New York, that was fun. The dinners. The galas with Ryan. When I was his escort to those events, everyone was all over me. But you gotta go home. At home I felt like I was part of some fringe group, and not even your fringe group. Until that night in England. Oh and a night at Pride Week in D.C." He recounted an experience in the Capital. "I got on a metro train, and I realized it was packed with gay men from all over the country, including small towns. As I eavesdropped on that train, I realized that these were just guys, state employees, tech guys, mechanics who'd found the courage to come out of the shadows, to come to D.C. for Pride, and to continue to live in their little towns. To move away from the margins. On that train, I found it, too."

Jim let his hair down. He dated some cool guys and he seemed, well, less judgmental in general. Previously, though he had loved my crew of creative misfits, they had sort of scared him. Now he embraced them. Jim finally seemed to get that on this crew, relationships developed deep and fast.

He was palpably more confident with whom I hired and how I saw them fitting into the crew. He even saw me serving at times somewhat of a paternal role in their lives rather than suspecting that I hired handsome guys only because I had ulterior motives. Despite his shift in understanding, Jim was concerned that I was getting in too deep with one young and very lost young man in particular. One day he pulled me aside and said, "Keep it professional with Kel. You are not his Daddy. You can offer him a good job but you cannot save him."

I had met Kel at Artbar. I sat down beside him because he had a sketch pad open and because he was a skinny punk with a botched, self-shorn, black crewcut. He shut the pad quickly when I spoke. But he engaged me in conversation. He was fascinated by the idea of a garden as a work of art. A few beers in, I knew he needed a job. And I thought that I could help channel his creativity into gardening.

"I can't drive. So I couldn't work over in West Columbia," he said.

"I'll pick you up in the mornings," I countered. "I bet someone else will take you home."

Soon enough, shy, lost Kel was in the morning carpool. Everyone loved the bone-thin, pale boy who worked like a horse. He had arranged for his "roommate" to pick him up after work in the Garden's parking lot. There were no chairs to sit in while he waited in the baking sun. So one day the crew moved some giant boulders under the lone shade tree in the parking lot area. From that point forward, young Kel would recline on a couch-sized dusty rock, sketching in the shade of that misshapen Chinaberry tree.

Sometimes on the morning ride to the Garden, Kel showed me some of his sketches. He was a morning mess. I never asked about the smell, as he gave himself a sort of spit bath in the car. I never asked why he didn't sleep. I just bought him extra coffee. I never asked about his sex life either, but I knew it was harsh.

One morning I knocked on his door. No answer. I went in to wake him and saw sketches and syringes on the floor. His friend was passed out on the couch, but there was no Kel. When his friend finally was able to speak, he said that Kel had been taken away in an ambulance the night before.

I found out a few hours later that Kel hadn't made it through the night.

I'd hoped finding a passion for art and plants would have been enough to save him. I'd lied to myself. For weeks after, the garden seemed like a hopeless construction site with burnt orange mud and clodded manure weighing down everyone's boots. We put our heads down and trudged on. We planted some huge magnolias and palmettos. Plants always cheer up plant people a bit. But even those trees looked raw and alone

———

By contrast, Jim was feeling newly alive, invigorated. Always the motivator, one day he said, "Set up a weekend trip to Atlanta and let's make sure everyone gets the vision now." He'd become compassionate toward the crew. It was like he got it now. He got that people could be different but still fit in. I used to think that he saw us as a bunch of oddballs. Now he was one of us — just a bunch of semi-lost folks gardening and having a beer in the pub.

20: Bonding on a Botanical Trip to Atlanta

In Jim's view, our crew of misfits needed exposure to other gardens. And it was true that most of the folks on the crew hadn't seen the new, cutting-edge gardens in nearby cities. So Jim directed me to set up an elaborate field trip to gardens in Atlanta so everyone could see great examples of private and public gardens.

We'd plowed through the drudgery of working on a winter construction site and Jim made the right call. We needed exposure and inspiration. But this trip had a lot of added pressure. Since arrangements had been made based on Jim's professional contacts in Atlanta, we needed to be on our best behavior. We needed to come across as professional among the staff of other botanical gardens.

The first day in Atlanta was stressful, but it worked. So after a quick motel shower, I was ready for a quiet happy hour. As I walked into the bar, Melodie's husband, Jimmy, was already there.

Jimmy was a redneck guy with long hair and just one ear. He was born that way. He had his hair pulled up and tucked under a cap. One uncontrolled lock looked like it had escaped, but really it hung strategically to obscure the blank spot on the side of his head.

When we had first met, I wondered if there'd ever be a connection between us. Jimmy was a man's man. He loved talking about women. He loved sports. But it became clear that he also loved people, and we became good friends.

I took the barstool to his left, since conversation was easier on his ear side. Choosing this side had become a habit. After you got to know him, you just sat on his left so he didn't have to read your lips. Like a reporter or a twin brother, Jimmy had a way of diving deep and fast into conversation. I ordered a whiskey and thought, "Please, Jimmy, give me five minutes with my drink before you bring up the kiss."

He looked through top-shelf bottles at my reflection in the mirror across the bar. I got ready for the gut punch. He was going to analyze something I'd done today. He liked to do that.

"Jenks," he said with a deeply contemplative voice. "Do you think all those gay cowboys thought I was gonna come down to the bar in a dress?"

"Oh my God. What are you talking about?" I fought the vision of this husky, hairy, church-going, country boy wearing a sundress into the Day's Inn bar.

"When I got in the elevator, I was carrying Melodie's dresses. There was a bunch of gay cowboys in there. I just said, 'Hey, where y'all from?' Then I realized I was totin' a dress, and I wondered if they thought I was one of them, but one that wanted to be a cowgirl."

When we had pulled the vans into the Day's Inn Midtown, the marquee proclaimed "Welcome Gay Rodeo!" In the parking lot, a sizable number of booted, smoking guys leaned on trucks with cattle horns mounted to the hoods. Inside, the confused bartender mixed Alabama's greatest hits with Madonna's Vogue.

Jimmy liked odd people. Our garden crew of misfits was definitely that, but we'd changed, too. After working on an isolated construction site together for months, we'd cut a mile-long path through gorges lined with massive granite, caves, and dwarf palmettos. We'd wheelbarrowed asphalt along the entire path. We'd made mountains of custom soil and craned three-ton palm trees over walls. Rain or shine, we'd take three breaks a day in a tiny construction trailer; share a cold port-a-potty; and sift chicken carcasses, flip flops, and babydoll parts out of mountains of municipal compost. This kind of work is hard and changes people. Our team of misfits did more than change. We bonded through a shared mission of building a flagship botanical garden.

From one-eared Jimmy to our truck driver, from our hippy-chick interns to our former hostage negotiator tool guy — each of us on this trip to Atlanta was delighted, or at least intrigued, with the bucking boys from a traveling gay rodeo.

My Manhattan arrived. Neat. The bartender turned the music up. Madonna belted out a command. "Don't just stand there! Let's get to it!"

Jimmy must have thought Madonna had given him permission to start in on me with the big question: "Do you think you embarrassed Jim today when that Atlanta Botanical guy kissed you on the lips in front of everyone? Melodie would have been jealous if he had kissed me. Was Pat jealous?"

"No, Pat doesn't care." I told him. "The only person it kinda bothered was me. I dated that guy last year. I thought we were gonna be the gay garden power couple of Southern Gardens magazine. Actually, it was just one night at a conference but in my mind, it was dating. Still, I wish he hadn't done that today in front of everybody."

"Don't worry about it," Jimmy said. "The volunteers don't care either. Melodie liked seeing you blush. How come there are so many gay gardener guys anyway?"

That question got me thinking and triggered memories of Orchid Dan, Butterfly Garden Jerry, and Holly Guy Mike. Just one year ago, they were roommates. Now, they were up there, out there, with the Uncles. For a moment, I felt a sort of closeness. Unity.

"You know there aren't that many of us in the South," I said. "I guess that's why we keep up connections. There were so many in Seattle."

Jimmy kept pushing. "What's Jim gonna say about all this? I mean, he's out of the closet and all, but is he gonna think that was unprofessional for you to kiss a man in front of everyone? He's been playing the boss role strong today. Is he gonna say you made this trip too gay?"

I was defensive. "I did not. How was I supposed to know about the cowboys at this hotel? I made this trip jam-packed with botanical gardens, nurseries, greenhouses, and plant people. Anyway, he's the one that added Ryan Gainey's garden. Talk about too gay."

Earlier that morning, we had stopped at one of the gayest gardens in Atlanta. It wouldn't have been on my list, but it was a luxury to get into Ryan Gainey's private garden. We walked a rough stone path toward a simple stone trough. Antique French watering cans were a major clue things might be a bit fancy here. On the woodland path, a treehouse peeked over the hellebores. Inside the 1940s glass conservatory, an oasis of sugar palms, nun's orchids, and spiral shampoo ginger surrounded an open shower. Like a movie set, lavender soaps and luffa sponges sat on a teak stool. Outside, a red cedar arbor dripped with Old Blush climbing roses. It was a spectacular balance of elegance with rustic human craft and nature, wild but curated.

To prepare for this amazingly complex garden, we'd all watched the BBC's mini-series Great Gardens of the World hosted by Audrey Hepburn. The BBC had chosen to feature only one US garden: Ryan Gainey's private garden.

But half the fun of this garden depended on the eccentric gardener. Ryan Gainey played his self-created role, a mix of Lawrence of Arabia, Auntie Mame, and three or four different folks from Gone With the Wind. He epitomized an old way to be gay. He wore smocks, a silver-and-turquoise brooch, a flowing scarf, and a floppy straw sun hat. He spoke with dramatic gestures and catty comments. It all communicated "I'm gonna be so gay that it won't do you any good to call me queer." Brashness as a survival technique protected many hairdressers, florists, band leaders, and designers throughout the South.

Immediately, I lumped him into the same group as the Uncles, even though he was still alive. Like me, Jim knew men who lived life in this admirable, difficult way. It wasn't Jim. In fact, I think it sort of scared him. Today, to distance himself, he talked only about plants and confined his touch to handshakes.

"Jim better not say that I made this trip gay," I blustered. "He's conflicted, even among this cool crew of folks. Did you notice that he put out a hand to greet Ryan rather than hug him? I bet that's different from when they greet each other alone."

Ryan respected Jim's choice to shake hands, but Ryan gave me a dramatic hug on departure. As he hugged me, he whispered a teasing reprimand. "You be careful on the streets of Atlanta. With those ripped jeans, some people will think you came here to pick up trash."

The Uncles loved it.

Other crew members, now showered and ready to explore, wandered into the bar. Sergio, a Brazilian artist with strong ties to the South, swaggered in, wearing only a Speedo and ready for the swimming pool. Jimmy whispered, "Jenks is that what you'd call a banana hammock? Would you ever wear a Speedo?"

Brynda — muscular, strong jawed, and strong willed — joined us and was followed by two young interns who were too young to be in a bar. No one messed with Brynda, who sometimes went by the more masculine name Bryn. As she approached the bar, she ordered two margaritas for the minors. The bartender, like most people, quickly sized her up and knew that it was smarter to do what Bryn said.

Jimmy sighed at her bare shoulders. "You think any man has ever touched those pure white boobs?"

I hoped Jimmy would linger quietly on that fantasy for a few minutes. No such luck. He came right back and said, "Don't tell Melodie I said that. You know I love her boobs."

Jimmy resumed surveying and analyzing our crew through the bar mirror. "Look at Mr. Porter. How did he work his way into a booth with two cowboys? I bet a year ago he wouldn't have even come into this bar, much less be chatting up the gay guys. What the heck could he be talking about with a couple of gay cowboys?"

I ordered a second drink. Jimmy looked across the bar and caught my eyes in the mirror. I knew what was coming. The Uncles had already been asking. Now it was Jimmy. "The South has changed, hasn't it? Do you and Pat really wanna leave? To go to Seattle? Or California? Or someplace cooler when the Garden opens?"

I still didn't know for sure if I was home for a while or home to stay.

The conversation veered when Jim walked up. "This has been just great. Now everyone gets the bigger picture of what gardens do. And we have our research honed in for the collection plant group. Let's have a big party for the staff and volunteers. It'll be a review, another thank you, and a goal-setting event for the final push."

I felt a pang of worry in my gut. I wasn't great at parties, and I hadn't nailed down a collection plant.

❦

21: A Gathering Place for Gardeners

Melodie and Jimmy with their new baby bought a house, then called to say that the place next door was for sale. They felt like family. Pat and I bought the place but it had one downside: it abutted a basketball court that attracted a rough crowd. Gunshots, angry midnight basketball games, and rocks through the windows became part of our more urban life.

In Melrose Heights the 1930s houses were small bungalows which had suffered through the 1970s. But the area had character and a bohemian feel. Our real estate agents advised against buying there. They emphatically said that it was a bad neighborhood, which was code for having too many Black people.

Mary and Pete lived directly across the street from us. They sat on their front porch all day — Mary usually in a floral house robe, and Pete with a Pabst in hand — and they watched the block better than any security guards might. Mary loved flowers, but she had a hard edge about her. Quiet, rail-thin Pete, looked down a lot when she talked. Mary loved flowers. Pete loved Pabst.

Their house stood out, partly because of Mary's taste in design. She grew purple heart, portulaca, and pony tail palms in concrete planters painted bright aqua blue. She liked to strategically place a few plastic flowers in the containers for more color. And Mary had concrete squirrels that seemed to scamper up the front of the house.

Mary introduced me to some of the old-lady gardeners in the neighborhood. I'd bring them extra flowers from work, so they ended up calling me the flower man.

Every day, when I pulled up after work, I knew Mary and Pete would offer me a Pabst. If I had an errand, I'd offer Pete a ride to his favorite fishing hole. Sometimes Pat would pick him up later, and he'd give us fresh, cleaned catfish. On those lucky occasions, Pete would cross the street with a bag of fish and beers, and sit with us talking about Mary, relationships, and the days of his youth when he was the first Black certified forklift technician in the state.

The decision to buy a house made my skull hurt. This was the commitment, the tie to this town, that I'd told myself would never happen. According to my original plan, I'd be leaving for Seattle in another three to six months. Instead, it seemed like I was giving up on a dream or trading it for something else.

Pat felt the same. Buying wasn't easy financially. But Jim Martin helped, reminding us that other people, richer people, buy and sell all the time. That made it seem less of a commitment.

———

Jackie, a charismatic mutt that had been a street dog, moved in. A creature of habit, he made it obvious that he needed to take morning trash can scouting trips around the entire block. We tied a bell onto his collar. Everyone knew him, and most loved him. In fact, we ended up meeting neighbors through Jackie, and soon most people on the block realized he belonged to the two White "brothers" who had just moved into the neighborhood.

Pete and Mary, as well as a good number of others, referred to Pat and me as brothers. We rarely felt the need to explain. However, I remember a gentle, redneck construction guy, who was refinishing our floors. He said, "Y'all brothers? Nice that you can still live together."

I thought that this guy needed to know who's paying him, so I gathered my courage and corrected him. "Look at us, man. He's practically Irish. We're not brothers. He's my boyfriend."

That country-boy contractor smiled and said, "Oh I see where you're coming from."

He just needed to know the right word.

I did most other renovation work myself. Alone. Pat didn't love that kind of work, and my terrible temper, directed at machines and falling plaster, scared him.

One room was always a dusty construction mess. In the other rooms, though, we set up house. The living room developed a luxe, thrift-store vibe with huge couches that came from Melodie's grandmother's estate. There were couches on the screened porch and a fire pit out back. Our home was easy, cozy, and quickly became a gathering spot for the garden crew.

———

Porter came early and brought Jim Beam, a cooler of beer, and a box of vegetables from the farmers market. For an hour or so he'd watch me do something like paint the bathroom ceiling. He'd talk the whole time about plants, especially collection plant ideas, or something he wanted to do but not alone like get tickets to see Aerosmith. He would punctuate his conversation with little one-liners: "Steven Tyler is a beautiful man even when he's dressing like a woman."

Then I'd shower and start supper as folks filtered in. Since Porter had been in the Army decades ago, he and my officemate Jack had lots in common. Jack always brought his compact and ever-engaging wife, Jung.

Jung cooked Korean food for us and taught us about using rice cookers. "No measure cup! Just put the rice in. Put your hand on top, and fill the water to your knuckles. It's the only way that works!"

"But our fingers are different sizes," I objected.

It didn't faze her. "No matter," she said. "It's always up to the knuckles."

She also taught us to make what became a favorite snack: cold sweet rice in fried tofu skin.

Pat brought a whole different kind of diversity to our house. His reporter friends hailed from across the country. They often joined us and some even dropped their children off with us occasionally.

Pat's writing work was focusing more and more on investigative journalism. He was fascinated by the revitalization of some small towns around the state. Empty store fronts suddenly had signs in Spanish as a new labor force moved into the state, Mexican immigrants, started to impact small town life. Pat's stories on this change ended up bringing interesting Spanish speakers to our house, for an evening or sometimes for days.

Bob and Eric were there frequently, too. Eric worked nearby, downtown in the old prison. That prison building was a foreboding, four-story granite block monolith built in 1886. It held the state's electric chair, and physically loomed over the new canalside park while metaphorically looming over the entire town.

Eric came by late one afternoon to drop off some plants. We talked about how both of our houses now had a constant flow of people. "Sometimes I need a little quiet," I told him.

Eric didn't give advice directly, but he always had some story with a point that he meant for me to figure out on my own.

"You know, at work all the men are lifers. They have to figure out how to live together. There's a group of transexuals. Some of them made up an impromptu softball team. Only trans folk. They play in cut-off prison pants and tie shirts above their bellies and call themselves The Daisy Dukes."

I thought he was joking and said so: "You're making this up. My prison guard tool guy at the Garden never told me that."

"But he knows," Eric continued. "Everybody knows that it's best to let people be themselves. Even there, everybody needs to feel at home."

I had now lost my cherished alone-time, but this new house felt like home. A whole lot of people, some of whom I didn't even know, would end up sleeping on the couches, the screen porch, or the futon.

Often reporters, guest speakers, and other botanical garden folks would come for parties. Local horticulture students would join, too. Once J.C. Raulston sent a carload of students who spent a few nights while I was out of town. Unfortunately, the A/C broke while they were there, but they were all happy to sleep on the porch and deck.

A mentor from Seattle decided to spend the whole summer. On his second day in town, he met a beautiful plant salesman, a Black guy with dreadlocks and Rasta look. That guy ended up staying all summer, too.

Jim liked being here, too. But sometimes, the constant flow of strangers was bit too much for him. If he had a professional guest or a speaker in town, he'd try to figure out if they'd like the vibe at my house. If they were more formal, we'd go to Jim's on-trend, fancy house for sit-down dinners with china and a few local A-list gay guys.

———

I kind of knew the Uncles hoped I'd aspire to that more refined lifestyle. But they pretty much approved of our opium den ambiance, and they loved the flow of young gypsies and endless turntable music: Liza with a Z, Pansy Division, and Wheels on a Gravel Road.

The Uncles now included Willie. He immediately moved into our new house with us. We brought Willie's washtubs: the navy blue enameled insides of washing machines. They'd been his favorite planters. They fit right into the neighborhood, and now held the Christmas tree bamboo that had sprouted through the deck where Pat and I had our first date.

People who came to visit usually brought plants, as gardeners always do. Lots of these plants would make me wonder where they had been my whole life. Others would make me question why I'd never noticed them before because they'd always been a part of my childhood, in my woods and garden.

The garden rooted in and reflected the inside of the house. Eclectic, full of life, and often full of interesting people.

Pat and I were figuring out how to weave together a colorful, comfortable life in a small town — a place folks had warned us not to move to and in a neighborhood where folks had told us not to move. We were making a family, a real home on our terms.

Everybody needs to feel at home.

22: Apologizing with Sparkly Jello

One morning, Melodie, Jim, and I took a dawn walk through the Zoo then retreated to our old attic office for a volunteer party-planning meeting. But we never got to the party planning. I watched Jim sort through the mail while his face contorted and he grumbled things like, "I can't believe this." It seemed some folks in Admin quickly pushed through some policy changes. These big-picture changes affected Jim directly. He left without saying a word. Mad.

By our regular 10 a.m. meeting, he was taking his anger and frustration out on me. He adamantly rejected my proposed planting for some out-of-the-way beds. My combination of Mexican bamboo and Spanish yucca would have been spectacular, but he said, "No. I understand the texture and form would contrast nicely. But no. I think all of your plant choices have a deeper problem. They do not make any attempt to bring us flowers. You focus on weird plants while we need pretty things that our guests can relate to."

I could hear Admin's words in his voice. Someone up the chain demanded flowers. Flowers, flowers, and more flowers. The higher-ups didn't care about serious plantings or cutting-edge horticulture.

But I wasn't backing down. "We're supposed to show the public beauty beyond petunias and shasta daisies. Or that coarse-leaved, trashy-red swamp hibiscus." This was an intentional provocation. I knew he'd take that as an attack. He loved the lanky, scarlet *Hibiscus coccinius*.

The day went downhill from the meeting. Melodie tried every last one of her middle-child-soothing techniques to make us play pretty again. I bucked up, and Jim barked orders. Back in the office he told me to schedule a weekly meeting for the three of us to review the core collection search and Museum grant. "Jenks, you're letting the Museum grant work slide, and I need more input. The whole grant expires soon, and then they won't pay for the consultants' airfare. And I've bought tickets out of my pocket for the guy from Chicago Botanic and San Francisco Botanic."

I'd met both of those men before. Jim could have used their names, but he was not-so-subtly reminding me of the national reputation stakes of this project. It was like all the good work I knew I had done was vanishing. I tapped loudly on my keyboard. He added, "You will get this right."

"I could get this right," I mumbled, "if you'd let me focus. But today, what am I doing? Making dessert for your volunteer party. Why can't you do that? Or some caterer that you use for your high-tone parties?"

Melodie stood up, "Let's just walk outside for a few minutes, OK?" But Jim was totally pissed at me. He practically yelled as we went down the office stairs, "Go home. Melodie and I will set up for the volunteer party. You go home. Be back at 6 pm. With dessert for 20. It better be delicious."

———

My VW didn't have air conditioning anymore, so driving just made me hotter. I drove through an empty, sad downtown where not one person walked the streets except an old farmer, literally in overalls, coming out of Hinson's Feed and Seed. In the middle of downtown, you could buy chickens, 50-pound bags of every animal food, bales of hay, and bulk turnip seeds. Downtown didn't have one cool thing. Granted there was one spiffy restaurant out of my range and a members-only gay bar, but mostly there were smoky-windowed banks, a uniform shop, and an entire store devoted to boiled peanuts. There was no coffee bar, no decent real bar, and most importantly, no grocery store. On the way to my house, I passed a few college bars, a drive-up ice cream stand straight out of 1950, and several ratty bungalows that had the same centipede front yards with azalea hedges. Every other house had a lanky gardenia bush whose flowers may smell exotic, but the leaves were always yellow and looked like they were dying.

My coming back here to South Carolina now seemed to have been a huge mistake. Jim didn't really want me at the Garden. He wanted someone more conventional. I couldn't toe the line to make him look good to Admin. Admin wanted a Yes Man. The garden club ladies saw me as an interloper. Melodie was settling into the inertia of family life. My friends back in Seattle were right. This was wrong.

Once I was home, I was surrounded by the hum of the window unit AC and the dial-up screech as I signed onto AOL to look for jobs. I pulled out a decent bottle of mescal to get a little drunk.

Boxes of kitchen stuff sat unopened. Not my stuff. I didn't have stuff. Robert, now buried in New Orleans, had arranged to have boxes of kitchen supplies shipped to me after his death. I could picture him, skin and bones, covered with lesions, and all the while giggling as he imagined me opening boxes of pretentious tea sets and unwrapping crystal champagne coupes. He had everything inventoried, and that inventory was a vocabulary lesson in the decorative arts. It took me hours of inventory work to figure out what 24 coupes were.

I'm sure The Uncles welcomed Robert warmly into their group. When I need them, or they need to say something, I see them all together. They're standing in a haze, like the gay rat pack, leaning in and offering advice. I can pick Robert out easily. He's the one wearing a Russian shapka, ear flaps down, braving the chill of a Seattle summer, and with his martini glass slightly, only slightly, raised in salute. A high-handed toast would be tacky. But never mind the shapka.

A car door slammed outside. It was Porter. Melodie must have called him. He walked in with purpose. "Well, if that's what Jim wants you to do, he's the boss. If the Zoo wants to hire you from halfway across the country."

I interrupted, "All the way across!"

"Look. If they're going to just let your plant knowledge sit and smolder, then they just don't know what they are doing. I tell you what," he shook his pinkie ring. "I won't be giving them a single penny of a donation. Not one more cent."

Porter let me vent for a while. He listened to me contemplate moving on.

At one point, he reiterated, "They don't know what they have, but they'll see what they had when you're gone."

This struck me as something you'd say to a child, and I realized that as a high school teacher, he had probably done this entire scenario but with teenagers. Was Porter using his teacher's psychology tricks on me?

He picked up a crystal champagne coupe and changed the subject. "You know when I was a boy, we didn't come up here. This part of town was nice, green, and clean. A block away, the road went dirt. This part of town was a world away from the mill."

"Look at you now, Mr. Porter! You drive your Lincoln over here to cheer up guys like me in what has become the low-rent part of town. Look at this place. There's a street drain right out there, at midnight, tens of thousands of two-inch-long cockroaches boil up from it so thick I couldn't walk to the Eats diner even if I wanted to. Despite all of that, I like the trees over here. Don't get me wrong, I like it here. And I like that we brought Willie's jungle with us."

Porter saw an opening, "The old man taught me a lot. Even when I wasn't ready for some of it. You know that some of the volunteers really support you and want you to be at this party tonight. The big boss Satch will be there, too. We could just walk in for a few minutes."

I disconnected AOL and said, "OK, Porter. I get your point. Let's go get some brownie mix. I have to make dessert for 20 people."

"No need. I brought something easier. Something my Granny made at Christmas. It's festive and Christmas fancy."

———

Jim, Melodie, and the crew had transformed the break room for the party. A massive, purple carpet covered the concrete floor; a dozen floor lamps with warm, dim bulbs stood on boxes and platforms; and a Barbra Streisand CD was playing at full volume. Huge flower arrangements covered the time clock. The place was transformed and ready for a party.

I walked in and was greeted with a very loud "There she is! Back from the dead!" Jim practically sang this. I knew it was his way of telling me we were OK. Then once he saw my tray, he was truly effusive.

"Is that real crystal? Mr. Farmer has crystal? Well, now! La-tee-da! That is really attractive."

I held a tray of 20 champagne coupes overflowing with golden cubes of sparkling jello. It looked like solidified champagne. Each tiny bubble, floating in the jello, sparkled in the dim lamp light. Porter's dead Granny's recipe, served in dead Robert's crystal, never looked so alive. The trick, Porter had taught me, was adding ginger ale at just the right moment so the jello solidifies around the carbonation.

We had fun making it. The idea of taking a country housewife party recipe, something old and disdained like Jello salad, and polishing it up appealed to me greatly. I could see the diamond in the lump of coal. A little light flashed in the sparkly jello of my mind. Maybe it was time to look beyond the cool new plants that I'd been trying so hard to use to impress people. Maybe it was time to look more closely at those country yards, the backwoods gardeners that Porter continued to take me to visit. Those folks hunkered down in their hot garden. They knew which plants were either born here or slowly got used to the tension of the South.

❦

23: Getting a Grip on the Core Collection

O n top of a sandhill, just past Piggy Park BBQ, Porter's garden featured lots of weird bulbs mixed among dwarf Sandhill oaks and prickly pear cactus. Grass would barely grow there. If plants did thrive there, they'd thrive anywhere. There was nothing elegant about the place — a country clapboard house with a well in the yard, concrete block stepping stones, and trees whose girths were double the black plastic pots they'd been potted in decades ago.

This evening, we stood in his sandy garden with beers and bug spray.

"How often has it flowered?" I asked about the plant growing close to the ground in front of us.

"Oh, just five or six times, but it grows leaves every year."

"Five times in forty years! Well, it's fascinating," I said, "but not a great garden plant. Definitely not a core collection candidate."

Porter nodded as he mused, and I caressed the wrist-thick, foot-tall Ammocharis stalk. It was a stubby thing, and on top of it were a hundred burgundy wires, each tipped with a wide-open, flesh-pink star. Six gray leaves laid out flat on the ground. I brushed away sand from under those leaves to find the top of a bald head buried underground. I imagined the remaining part with shoulders, and fingers holding on to the sand, deep down. A little more brushing away of sand revealed a crimped aluminum dog tag with *Ammocharis coronica* 1946 Sand Lily handwritten on its surface.

"It's special," Porter told me. "It was about the size of a golf ball when I got it. Back then my family went for drives every Saturday. My parents found a man in the Market Bulletin who was a plant collector down near Orangeburg. He had a backyard hobby nursery. I remember how I watched him right away. He was younger than Daddy, probably just back from the war. He had a black eye patch, a thick black mustache, and football-player-thick, hairy legs.

"I saw these four or five little bulbs in individual clay pots — brown golf ball bulbs pushing halfway out of the dirt. I was hooked. He said they weren't for sale and kept talking with my parents. After a while, I just knew that he knew. At the end of the day, he said, 'I tell you what; I'll sell you that rare bulb for one dollar, but it's not just a plant. It's a responsibility. Not only do you have to take care of it, but you have to learn its real name. When it flowers, I want you to take a picture and either write me a letter or bring me the picture."

"I did just that three years later, and he treated me like an adult. I continued to see him right up until I left for the army. He always had a rare bulb for me and always had an encouraging story. One time his "brother" was there. I knew that he was encouraging my interest in the plant world. And I knew he was encouraging me."

Whoa! Porter just came out to me with a few carefully chosen words. Damn, I wanted to hug him but the Uncles whispered, "Easy now, this is all new to him." So I said something in a very Southern way that acknowledged his revelation but didn't linger on it or delve into it: "Daddy used to say, 'You never forget the man who put you up on that mule for your very first ride."

————

Later on I planned a plant-buying road trip to Florida, stopping first in South Georgia to visit Pat Malcolm, an acquaintance of Porter and a respected but notoriously odd crinum breeder. Porter wanted more than anything to go along. And I love having a road trip planner and companion. As we drove 301 South into Georgia, we talked about this guy's homoerotic bulb catelog.

"Don't say anything about that," Porter warned me. "He plays Southern Gentleman farmer all the way. He has a family and he's very, very religious. Just keep your mouth closed about any of that."

Meeting that Southern gentleman crinum farmer wasn't easy at first. He drove us in his pickup around the flower fields, all under massive pecan trees. There was Porter in front, me in a tiny jump seat, a well-worn Bible on the dashboard. I felt like the farm boy. Mr. Malcolm even asked me to keep an eye on a child while he and Porter went to his breeding field.

When they returned, I gathered that something Porter said to Mr. Malcolm in private must have changed his tone. He ended up selling us some of his crinum bulbs, but more importantly, he gave me his number and told me never to order from the catalog. Instead, he told me to call him directly.

Malcolm's work with crinum offered an important perspective for me. In the mid 1900s, most crinum breeding took place in California and Texas where dry summers impacted plant performance and pests. Here, in the South, I'd found a professional resource who could offer rare plants as well as flowering time, size, and growth rate. And he was just a few hours' drive from the new Garden.

Later, back in my VW Fox wagon, I asked Porter if he'd noticed the Bible on Mr. Malcolm's pick-up dash. "Do you think he was stand-offish at first because he realized I'm gay? But then why would he warm up?"

Porter didn't answer directly. "He never asked about our wives or family. He knew what not to ask. He's like all the teachers at school and all the men at my church. They know, but they need to ignore it. It's what Clinton called it "don't ask, don't tell."

Porter was quiet for a while after that. Then he turned to me. "It's what kept me going to Charleston. You know what I used to say? 'Charleston. All cock and no commitment!'"

I about ran off the road into one of those black-water ditches full of alligators. The Uncles were right there, ready to catch me. They'd known all along. I guess, on some level, I had known, too. But that statement, which sounded something like what the Uncles might say, coming out of the mouth of this conservative old teacher, hit me hard. When I had regained my composure, I simply said, "Sir. Mr. Porter. If you'd be so polite as to explain."

Back during his teaching career at the high school, when other teachers talked about football games, church, or family, Porter talked about gardens and his plant friends from across the country. What was left unsaid protected his friends from being uncomfortable, and it kept them also from possibly having to reproach or reject or even fire him.

Plants shielded Porter from the injuries, insults, and injustices that were all too real for men of his age. As J.C. Raulston always said, "Plants won't hurt you." For Porter, plants did more than shield. They helped him hook up on the down-low.

On Friday afternoons Porter would head to Charleston. Its perfect array of famed gardens provided a secret gay getaway. By the time he got settled into a hotel, sailors, cadets, businessmen, and hustlers, having finished their suppers, went for a walk on the Battery. It was the ideal place to meet strangers, as guys would lounge on the sea wall. These beautiful men would stretch, exercise, and generally show off. You could ask for directions or offer a smoke to a stranger, and it would often serve as an invitation for something more.

"Have the time?" could be interpreted in different ways. Charleston was a dark and dirty Navy town back then. White Point Gardens and The Battery offered cruising in public areas. It was perfect if you knew the signs and signals. If Porter ran into someone he knew, he could say, "I just walked down from the motel to see if the camellias were blooming."

Occasionally he would walk along Murray Boulevard over to West Street and the warren of streets packed with sailor bars and brothels. He'd never go inside. According to a friend, even the police wouldn't go into those places. If he ran across the right sailor on the street, they'd walk into the darkness and find a quiet spot to be alone.

His room at the Francis Marion hotel, which was a bit tattered and cheap then, was only a place to rest and a base from which Porter would actually do some garden tours in the daytime, then find another sailor that night.

Come Monday morning he was back in the teachers' lounge at his high school with cover stories about the glorious gardens of Charleston.

"See what I mean?" Porter quipped. "It was perfect for me. Charleston back then was all cock, no commitment."

Once Porter opened up, he really opened up. After his Charleston revelation he let loose on the genteel society of our town and the pretentiousness of elitist gardens. His frustration spilled right over into the pitfalls of about every single plant we had considered for the core collection. It became apparent that Porter had listened to every word that passed between Jim, Melodie, and me.

We drove the backroads, stopping at Chez Suzanne, Bok Tower Gardens, and every nursery on the way to Port Charlotte, with a special stop to see a young crinum breeder in Tampa. As we focused more and more on crinum, other plants that I'd considered for collections simply dropped off the list.

After our crinum stop in Tampa, we both wanted to go to Busch Gardens, the famed amusement park. We had to rent a space at the dog kennel to unpack and water all our plants before we could spend the broiling day in the creatively planted zoo and amusement park.

Porter talked. On the roller coasters, he talked. As we drove through the hilly cow lands of Ocala, he talked. And, of course, when we unwound for the night in some motel bar, he talked. It wasn't any different when we pulled into the Silver Slipper, a classic, old-school motel way out some abandoned highway. We were alone in the bar, and the owner made us Indian food. He put out a giant bottle of Indian beer and two plastic cups. As Porter talked, he told me about his days at college, years in the Navy, his few close friends, and his long pen-pal relationship with crinum growers across the country.

Somewhere west of Jacksonville, Porter put it bluntly, "Jenks, your collection plant really has to be crinum."

"But we need a strategy," I exclaimed to Porter. "Melodie and Jim will buy in to the crinum thing for sure." It made sense from climate, history, and garden standpoints. There was even a native crinum. But there was no comprehensive botanical collection in the Deep South. Porter knew what I was about to say: "But you know some fancy gardeners, the people who think of crinum as cemetery lilies, will be pissed off."

❧

24: Coming Out with Crinum

"**A**re y'all really planting milk-and-wine lilies? They are so lovely. But...."

I heard the meaning behind "they are so lovely." She might well have said, "They are different, aren't they?"

The southernism different was not a compliment. Then, of course, there was the but. Lots of the blueblood garden club members mastered the say-something-nice-before-you-ram-in-the-knife setup. This lady said my name like three interconnected syllables with a little flourish added at the end. She'd once asked, "Jenks, is your grandmotha in the D.A.R.?"

Then came the transition. "They sometimes work well planted on graves. As would a more refined real lily. But...."

Now the declaration of contempt, the twist of the knife. "Are you sure they are really right for the Botanical Garden?"

I started my justification. She shut it all down. "They do remind one of the country. You know that some people say they are Black people's plants." She said the last part in a low and hushed whisper.

She read the shock on my face. "I don't mean that in a racist way. Of course, you might see them in the gardens of country White people, or as Mother would say, 'po' bukra.'"

I dismissed her disapproving words. They were irrelevant to me and offensive. With Jim's approval and with the blessing of the three garden directors who'd soon be here to review our choices via the Museum Assessment Grant, we were on track for all the approval we needed.

Three long months of work was finally culminating in the seal of approval from three prestigious garden directors. I felt like it was a win and a relief. I could finally stop considering aspects of other plants and get down to building a core collection of crinum.

We wrote press releases and started a more organized system of collecting from old gardens and purchasing from specialty breeders. We started laying out plans and executing a solid process for working with a core collection.

Almost immediately we faced a problem — sourcing crinum. We needed big bulbs in big numbers. Even into the mid-1990s, no one could find them in a garden center, in a suburban landscape, or in city public plantings. You could order small bulbs in small numbers from mail-order sources, but those tiny bulbs would take five or more years to come to flower. To solve our dilemma, we took lots of road trips to wherever we heard we could find mature crinum. We engaged in weekly "shack botany," searching for remnant crinum at abandoned houses, cemeteries, and gardens. We also traveled to the very few botanical gardens that had been growing crinum to see if they could spare any bulbs.

One Saturday morning, way out in the small town of Branchville, South Carolina, Porter and I spotted a few crinum lilies flowering beside an abandoned store. Seeking permission, we walked next door into Smoak's Barber Shop. I whipped out my business card. Since everyone in the state and their grandchildren had been to Riverbanks Zoo, that card carried a lot of weight. Mr. Smoak said the building next door wasn't his, but he reckoned it'd be fine if we looked around.

We thanked him for the information and walked out. In no time, I was squatting to set up a tripod by the abandoned store when a beat-up blue pickup roared up. A strapping, shirtless, redneck guy, 35 years old or thereabouts, jumped out and yelled, "What are y'all doing on my property?"

We were trespassing. His dust and bluster would have scared me if I'd been alone, but former teacher and principal Porter had taught, paddled, and mentored guys like this for decades, including one from this neck of the woods. In a quick minute, the young buck all settled down as he recognized the connection and blurted out, "Yes Sir, that was my uncle. You're the one that made him swallow a wad of chew?"

We were in, and he was ready to tell us about those lilies. "Let me ask you this. Why won't they die? I've been running the mower over them and even spraying Roundup on them. For years. Years! Roundup oughta kill 'em. I just want to be able to cut the grass there. You want those? Help yourself. Dig all you want. What kind of lilies are they anyhow?"

We filled up the back of Porter's big pick-up. We'd drawn a crowd. Mr. Smoak and some guy getting a shave in the barbershop came over to watch. The guy said, "There's a bunch out in the swamp. My Momma pulled 'em up out there. She called 'em swamp bells. Are you going to plant 'em in the Zoo?"

I wanted to know the story of swamp bells, but it would have to come much later. We had digging to do.

———

Road trips back in the day started with a phone call, or a paper map, or sometimes even a mailed letter. Porter had good contacts. He'd been part of the American Bulb Society since the 1950s. His subgroup carried on a round robin. A dozen or so folks from around the country would mail photos of their crinum, each adding notes and comments. Person A mailed to person B, and so on until finally, the initiators would get back their photos with opinions and often a request for a bit of the plants.

Porter had talked to these folks on the phone but had never met them. Since there was a concentration of the group in Texas, Porter and I planned a trip. Pat joined us for fun. This was Porter's first time on a plane since he was in the military in the 1950s. Pat was working on stories about the new influx of Mexicans settling in and revitalizing some small towns in South Carolina. A few days in San Antonio could be informative for him.

In her plywood-sided house that baked in the East Texas sunshine, Marcelle Sheppard poured us all iced tea. The window unit hummed as she pulled out her cellophane-covered photo books. There wasn't a single family picture in them. Instead, Marcelle showed us album after album of crinum she'd bred. She had two leatherette covered albums for her canna lilies, too. Unlike all the older male collectors Porter introduced me to, Marcelle spoke to me like an equal right away.

She didn't tolerate pretense. She was certain of what she'd done and didn't need to mark her territory. Like a lot of plant people who are beyond trying to impress, she asked who I knew and who I'd traded plants with. Of course, her old friend Porter was with me, but we talked about Malcolm in Georgia and the young crinum guy I'd become friends with in Tampa. After that visit, Marcelle and I became friends, too.

After that initial meeting with Marcelle, we continued to drive west to see Linda Gay's crinum collection at the Mercer Arboretum in Houston. We stopped to see the famous former South Carolinian, John Fairey at Peckerwood. Then we went on to see the undisputed leader of crinum collections, young Steve Lowe, one of Marcelle Sheppard's proteges.

On that trip, Steve was the curator at San Antonio Botanical Garden, and he had deep crinum roots. Steve and I had in common serious crinum collector mentors from the Great Generation, and we both liked the idea of learning and passing on their love of crinum.

After that immersive trip I joined the letter-writing world and found people across the country who were happy to mail bulbs to me. I became penpals with Les Hannibal, the man who had written the book on crinum. Despite being in his late 80s, he became an enthusiastic penpal. He was old enough that he'd been mentored by bulb lovers of the late Victorian era. A stickler for details and propriety, he agreed to sell me one of the very last copies of his book. It and the bulbs I got from him were treasures.

Each letter arrived painstakingly typed on white, tissue-thin paper. His attention to detail and presentation were astounding. He typed, then re-read, painted on correction fluid, and retyped to fix the smallest mistake. Obsessed with the entire Amaryllis family, Mr. Hannibal kept every letter, paper, catalog, photograph, and scribble in the ten boxes and 200 folders which now make up a special collection at the University of California. I loved getting letters and plants from this true renaissance gentleman.

———

Word was now out across the South that we were building a crinum collection for the new Garden. Suddenly this plant that had seemed difficult to find started to arrive in a torrent. Every time I turned around, somebody's uncle, second cousin, or yard man had a really rare one with an amazing story.

Seeds arrived from wild collections in South Africa, Korea, and China.

I had to learn to refine our goals and to say no sometimes. A curated collection has goals and limits, and most importantly, it must be understood and managed. It's not about having one of everything.

Dale Peace, at Desert to Jungle in Los Angeles, tried hard to get me to take home the seed of her fifteen-foot-tall crinum 'Queen Emma'. As much as I loved her and the massive plant, Queen Emma doesn't make it through the South Carolina winter without protection. I had to say no.

A collector in Winter Haven, Florida, wanted to give us dozens of aquatic crinum. One of them lived in the mud on the bottom of a pond, sending up floating flowers almost like a water lily. He grew them in blue tubs of water. We didn't have water gardens, and I couldn't see a way that we could care for these. I had to say no.

A Cambodian friend brought me a rare, yellow crinum from Australia, admitting, "I snuck this in from my trip!" Seductive. But no.

In old cemeteries throughout the state we repeatedly found what we came to call Floppy White. I'm sure that its pure white flowers inspired folks to plant it in cemeteries. In European history, true lilies represent death and rebirth. They're often depicted on tombstones. True lilies, however, often rot in South Carolina, so white crinum makes a good stand-in. This particular one simply doesn't stand. It's pretty, but not standing upright means it will not appeal to the modern audience.

Enter our research mission. To put it bluntly, research can be involved and costly. For example, we could have chosen to investigate which American moths pollinate African crinum. We didn't go in that direction. Jim Martin's early directive was our guide: Riverbanks was not to be a center of funded research, but was to be a center that appealed to gardeners.

Our modern audience at Riverbanks wanted easy-to-care-for, rewarding plants. Discovering them would be the driving force behind our research projects. We got creative with plant combinations and testing crinum in various soils and brightness. We compared, photographed, promoted, and shared the best of the best.

Our education aspect was built around sharing and encouraging, or as Jim would say: "Use those crinum in ways that show the average visitor the beauty that you see." I did that and wrote about crinum. I gave presentations at regional conferences, local garden centers, and even at meetings of the American Association of Botanical Gardens.

A common pattern of resistance began to be voiced by other botanical garden managers. They pushed back and said that it was too cold for crinum where they garden. I heard this over and over from D.C. to Nashville to Saint Louis. As a result, we decided to augment our education strategy and started to send out gift bulbs to zoos and gardens with strings and cards attached asking for them to keep us posted on how the bulbs grow in their zone. Our preservation and conservation aspects were limited by resources. This sort of behind-the-scenes work in museums often is.

We ended up framing preservation as collecting stories and photos of a specific plant's history. Every story got collected and put in the database. For example, the swamp bells that Porter and I had collected near the Edisto River had a story. Plants from Marcelle had stories that often focused on the history of a family who'd carried bulbs around and cared for them, for generations.

Another part of preservation and conservation involved working with the local herbarium to provide dried, pressed flowers as well as accurate plant descriptions to be stored in perpetuity in the University of South Carolina science department.

The effort of choosing crinum for Riverbanks' core collection quickly revealed the rebel nature of our entire staff. We enjoyed the type of controversy that flew in the face of the sentiment of the woman who had called crinum Black people's plants or "po' bukra" plants. We savored the win of choosing a commoner's plant over those long-admired camellias and azaleas. Crinum may never win the hearts of the "cultured" Southern gardeners, but at least those people were thinking, reacting, having emotional responses, and remembering bits of history simply by seeing our plants.

One morning a tour group from Columbia College, a local women's college, followed me around. Before I got to my spiel on collection plants, a very Southern, blond, and sporty-looking woman piped up, "My grandmother had those."

I asked if anyone knew the flower's name. Immediately a Black woman said, "I don't remember their name, but my grandmother had them, too."

That same afternoon, on a Master Gardeners' tour I was conducting, an Indian woman said, "These are your lilies? My grandmother had them."

We were building bridges, making connections, and engaging all sorts of people. Maybe we'd even change the minds of some of those old garden snobs who disdained crinum. We were taking this old country plant and showing it off in a new Southern garden setting.

25: Freaking Out at the Black Tie Garden Gala

Towering flower arrangements and a forest of pastel-painted bare bamboo trees sparkled with lights. White tablecloths dulled the noise of the crowd and the clinking of silver. Champagne flowed. A quintet from some symphony orchestra played in the foyer of the brand-new Visitors Center. What had been our garden crew's private enclave, our construction site, had been transformed for the first-ever, black-tie Garden Gala.

This was exactly the kind of event that made me tense. I recognized that the feeling was tinged with resentment too. Weeks before this event, Jim had tried to ease my anxiety. He had reminded me, and most of the Garden crew, that this would be our party and an opportunity to reveal the fruits of our labor.

Jim, however, wanted us all dressed up for the gala. During the days before the event he had subtly reminded me that I needed to behave like I fit in. I knew he was right, so I gave myself many talks about trying to enjoy the party, to mingle with everyone, to share stories, and to quash my discomfort. I thought I could do all that. But I wasn't entirely sure I could pull it off.

The night finally arrived, and I found myself looking across the sparkling crowd of Columbia's big-money families, donors, and, of course, all of the garden club ladies. There were lots of black dresses, pearls, and silk. I noted a few sparkly dresses, too. Gentlemen flashed antique cufflinks — probably handed down from their war-hero grandaddies.

Jim had put together massive flower arrangements that qualified for being over-the-top floral art installations. His towering creativity along with access to a garden full of flowers transformed the space with huge floral swags, each hung floor to ceiling. These weren't greenery swags like some florist might have done, but more like living ropes of purple canna leaves woven with gold variegated giant reeds. Peach ginger lilies bunched together on tables like a bad, frilly tux shirt. Even the men's room sported masculine, 3-foot tall brass vases, holding 5-foot burgundy crinum lilies that soared over men's heads.

I stood in a corner with the caterer, feeling a bit like a squirrel in the rafters surveying the crowd. Four major cliques were here, and they mostly laughed in their little clutches while a few connectors, those social-butterfly types, fluttered around, mixing things up. Three of these cliques were in their element: the donors, garden club ladies and our own Administrators. But the fourth group, the fish-out-of-water group, was made up of us gardeners. Even though this was our home, somehow we didn't feel like it was our Garden anymore.

Most of us had never been to a black-tie event. Thank goodness our volunteer Betty had thrown a few formal dinners for us earlier in the year. Tonight Betty floated among the largest group, the blue blood group. The older gentlemen in their even older tuxes knew her as Colonel Dozier's charming wife. I read her motions when she was with them — social hugs, cheerful laughs, delighted surprise, sincere concern. She knew how to convey it all, even in a loud room like this.

I knew that Betty was wearing her put-together, social face. But when she looked across the room to our group, that facade melted, and she lit up as she saw spit-shined Jack and his wife Jung in her simple Korean silk dress, Brynda in her "sister-power" forest green tux, and me looking like a Lawrence Welk escapee in my white tux. We did look great. Tans make evening clothes look better, even if they're farmer tans.

I spotted my Daddy. He was out of his element too, wearing a poly-blend blue jacket and what I knew was a clip-on tie. The thought crossed my mind that my discomfort here was kind of his fault. He had reveled in being a black sheep, in raising me on a country farm growing turnips and caring for calves rather than giving me the kind of social exposure that would have placed me in this room at ease. In one way, though, the farming and dirt experience led me to my plant passion and my career, which put me in this room.

I continued to survey the crowd, wondering if all the glitzy people could read my discomfort. I wondered, too, if they suspected we gardeners had planned a quick escape to meet up shortly at our favorite bar.

After a moment I glanced over at Jim. He was different. But he was one of us too. We were all here because of him. We all wanted to see Jim in his element and enjoying his success.

My attention slowly drifted to the group of super donors and board members. I knew a few of them. I told myself that I should go over and talk to them. But I couldn't bring myself to do it. I stuck with the gardeners.

One of the gardeners was looking across the room and said, "They can't imagine the sweat and poop that was here yesterday."

I agreed. And I also thought that they couldn't imagine the sacredness of this space, the place where our beautiful garden family had been born.

Suddenly Jim was at my side grabbing my arm and whisking me through the crowd while Pat followed along as best he could, smiling all the while. Jim was intent on parading me around to this and that donor and saying, "Y'all know Jenks? He grew the crinum in the men's room!" or "Y'all met when we took the ladies down to the river and they got stuck!"

The Garden crew was luckier than I was. Some of them milled through the room on their own terms. They often found themselves mixing with the Garden Club Ladies. It was easier. At least, the crew and I knew their names; we'd taken them on enough Garden tours.

On Gala night those ladies held our arms and said, "I want you to meet my husband!" One said to me, "Y'all are so smart to have done this!"

They were proud of us, but occasionally I did feel like a trinket to be shown off.

But, in reality, the relationship was a two-way street. The Garden Club Ladies were brokers; they had the money to hire the talent. We were the talent, and they wanted to show us off. But I came to realize that we had our plant expertise, while they had their checkbook expertise and their own garden dreams. These women had wanted something amazing for Columbia horticulture for decades. This was just a big exchange of energy — their encouragement and support for our skills and muscle. Everybody played a role.

My favorite Garden Club lady, Emily, gave a little come-hither motion from across the room. She still wanted me to meet her son. As I angled my way through the crowd to her, I noticed another major group, Jim's A-list gay friends. These were the glowing men with bourbon cocktails who looked like they'd stepped out of GQ. The Uncles were probably over there. They hung around with the lipstick lesbian crowd. Some of them were the adult children of the other older crowds. Some of them I knew and liked a lot. Some of them I simply knew.

During the party Jim's friends did their best to pull Pat and me into their conversation. We hadn't tried hard to fit in over this past year. But I truly wanted them, especially Jim, to have a fantastic time and to remember this as the most elegant black-tie gala ever.

Pat and I stood still in the middle of the room as a parade of faces and chitchat flowed around us. I found my groove, telling harrowing stories about construction and my dreams for the garden. Casual, brief, entertaining stories. I actually got into it.

But Jennifer, one of the Garden crew, came up to me with a concerned look on her face. She said, "Jenks, you've been standing right here in this spot smiling and chatting for over an hour. It's like you're in a receiving line at a wedding."

She handed me a fresh drink and ordered me to meet her outside at nine. I had watched Jennifer transform from a privileged young student to a hard-working, compost-slinging, detail-oriented gardener. But tonight she was in her element. I knew that she had been raised in cocktail culture and knew not only how to navigate the scene but also how to use the all-important escape tactics in her repertoire. As she turned to walk away, she whispered in my ear, "When it's time to meet me outside, just say you want to go out and see the Garden at night and that you'll be right back."

"Good plan," I said. "Then we'll blow this place and meet at the brewery."

Jennifer smiled and responded, "I'll get the word to Melodie, Jimmy, and the rest of the gardeners."

––––––

As the appointed hour approached, Pat and I found Porter and his date and started moving slowly toward the door. Porter, his flashy date, Pat, and I had all arrived together in a rented Lincoln Town Car, gaudily gold. Porter's date, who had over-the-top tastes, had arranged everything for the four of us to have a glam evening. I'm pretty sure he had his own set of Uncles.

He had decided that we should all wear matching white tuxes with frilly white shirts. It felt like prom to me, and I knew those damned tuxes would somehow be a problem. And sure enough, they were.

We were almost out the door when a photographer from Columbia Metropolitan Magazine accosted us with a commotion and said, "Hold up fellas. Y'all are the entertainment, right? I need a photo of all y'all standing together."

Being called "the entertainment" struck me wrong. It offended my country-boy sensibilities and triggered all my squirrel-in-the-rafters, outside-the-clique feelings.

Porter felt me buck up and tried to defuse the situation. "We're not part of the Quintet! We're better for your magazine!" he said with fake cheerfulness. "This is the man who built the Garden, and you sure do need a photo of us all!" He held my shoulders and pushed me a bit forward.

We posed. I didn't smile. The photographer was about to take another picture, when he stopped, looked around, and then said, "Hey, one more thing. Could you call your wives over so we can get them in the photo, too?"

I don't know what I said exactly, but the photographer was lucky I didn't deck him. His statement was a trigger for sure. I heard all his old-school, good-ol-boy Southern prejudice in the assumption that we were all just alike, all playing on the same team, that we needed wives to make the photo better.

"Jenks," Porter said in a calming, low voice as he placed a hand on my arm. "This old man shoots a dozen galas a year. In this little town, rest assured, the men he usually shoots are all straight. Or have decades of experience playing like they are. He's just using his tried-and-true tricks to get people to smile so he can get a good photo and go home."

"We don't have wives," Porter said turning to the photographer and said, "We don't have wives. This is like a double date. Definitely a Who's Who couple photo. You'll probably need all our names for the caption, won't you? Hand me your pad."

As we walked away, I realized that the picture would be in a magazine that I had never read. We'd probably be the first gay couples on its pages. And that the thousands of people who did read it would see that. And they'd see the Garden, our garden. It now belonged to them, too. That's who we'd made it for. We'd said all along that the Garden would not be an old-school elitist garden. It would be a garden to intrigue and inspire all sorts of people.

I was a little calmer as we walked out the doors onto an overlook above the fountain, a spot with a sweeping vista of the Garden.

It was no surprise that most of the gardeners were out there on the terrace. But I didn't expect to see Jim and some of his friends, the big boss from the Zoo, his wife, and a few Garden Club Ladies all taking in the scene and enjoying a little breeze. We all stood together looking through the bent palmetto, down the lighted canal, and through the crinum and sweet potato vines that were flanking the cascade flowing the length of the garden. Moon vines and pale antique roses glowed in the distance.

Pat and I stood at the center of the Garden overlook, taking in the vista with our backs to the crowd. We turned to each other and had a little kiss under the bent palmetto. I worried a bit that someone might think that the kiss was inappropriate. I was pretty sure that two men kissing wasn't something most of them had ever seen. But when we turned around, our own sweet moment got sweeter as we noticed all the folks were watching us and smiling. I finally got it. I understood that they were all happy that we were happy. There was magic in that moment. Times were changing. Worlds were merging.

26: Tropical Planting on a Extrodinary Level

When our smaller crew gathered in the work bay on mornings after the black-tie gala, it was all business as usual again. Work carts zipped out on their way to the shady end of the Garden.

Early morning sunlight in this part of the Garden shined on the expanse of what had become a sort of fantasy jungle. The Garden overflowed with a tropical exuberance made possible by the many plants Melodie had vetted during her years of trials in the Zoo.

Visitors loved it here. Reporters and professional guests came from across the South to see the new Garden and photograph its tropicissimo style.

One morning the walkie-talkie blared with the voice of someone from PR asking me to meet a reporter. "We have a reporter from the Charlotte Observer coming to you. Can you meet him at nine?"

As I was about to click a response, that PR person added, "Don't talk about convicts, please."

Melodie's voice then burst over the walkie-talkie, "He'll only talk about himself these days."

I knew it was a joke. Sort of. Due to the daily grind of our jobs, we were often separated by woods and river, so we didn't see each other much. I felt a loss of connection with her.

I met the reporter at the fountain and offered him a hat. The white-hot, searing summer sun fried heads.

Then I launched into presentation mode. "The climate and rich soil is what drew European planters here. They could grow rice, sugarcane, peanuts, and cotton. And these are the things that set us apart from Charlotte's slightly higher elevation. It allowed us to turn the Garden into a tropical paradise."

The press loved that little introduction. It had become my standard. From the fountain terrace, we looked over the garden.

"What inspired these giant bamboo structures?" the press would ask.

"Fun and necessity," I would say. "We're growing giant tropical vines, like wooly morning glory with leaves the size of dinner plates. It would crush anything less strong. You gotta match plants to structures."

Examples grew all around us. Young families walked under towering orange Mexican sunflowers woven through golden candelabra trees. A groundcover of native, running dune morning glory and 'Blackie' sweet potato vines carpeted over brick walkways, benches, and an entire fountain, too. Crinum erupted through the carpet of black sweet potatoes. Towering bananas, orange pagado clerodendrum, Cuban gold duranta, and cat whiskers sprawled out into paths.

Another time a curious reporter asked, "Did you use all these tropicals because they're trendy?"

I rolled my eyes, and forged a diplomatic response. "We'd rather lead than follow trends. And Melodie, our Zoo Horticulture Curator, has been working with these plants for years. We have been able to build our success on her groundbreaking trials."

I tried to remember in these interviews to credit Melodie with the work that she did before I had started at the Garden. Her work truly was groundbreaking, but she was always nonchalant and humble about it.

One morning on one of our Zoo walk-throughs, Melodie said, "We never dreamed that most of these plants would turn out to be perennial — Swedish ivy, Florida firecracker bush, and that coral vine. We were being a little lazy that first winter when we left those black-leaf xanthosoma. I thought they'd rot and die over winter. But in the spring they started coming up like little black hearts through purple pansies. Then, by the end of May, they were chest high, so I started trying other xanthosoma species in other exhibits."

Melodie and I wanted to push this work further. Jim loved the tropical look, too. He'd been advocating for it and had agreed to send me and Melodie on a buying trip to find new plants. With no woods or river to separate us, I secretly hoped that this trip would be a way for us to reconnect.

We rented a giant box truck and hit I-95, heading for the Florida line. We had only driven four hours south, but it felt like a whole different world. Florida had long been a place of escape and exploration for me, and now I was getting to share this experience with my old friend Melodie.

Melodie didn't love Florida. While the sun darkened me into a coffee tan, it had the potential to scorch and burn Melodie, so she protected her alabaster skin and baby-soft complexion with a big hat.

I dove into white-hot gravel lots where nursery plants huddled. She shopped the shade sections. She had her list of needs and wants as well as nurseries and botanical gardens to visit. I wanted to do her list and more, but we had only so much time. So one of the areas where I thought we could buy more time was to cut out time dedicated to our lunches.

Melodie caught wind of that and took to scolding me. "You're going to make us drive through Big K so as not to waste time for lunch? You know how to take all the fun out of everything."

The prospect of finding a way to reconnect was not looking all that good, particularly given that we seemed to operate at different speeds when traveling.

Later, back in the chillbox of a hotel room, I was getting ready to head out to meet new friends. Perhaps all this time together was actually starting to backfire. Then, out of the blue, Melodie turned to me and said, "You're leaving me in the hotel room tonight to meet some hot nurseryman you met this morning?"

She caught me off guard with her remark and stern face. For a moment I didn't know what to do or say. Then as I started to open my mouth, she burst out laughing.

She knew me too well. I would always jump at the chance to meet new plants and the people who were obsessed with them.

"I'm networking for us," I told her. "You know it's the after-hour plant walks and beers that lead us to getting meaningful connections and really rare plants."

As I walked out the door, she called out, "Bring back some scotch and Cheetos!"

We felt reconnected after our road trip. The new tropicals we'd collected went into the Garden or the Zoo or got cut in the Growing Center for propagation.

New visitors kept showing up to see the tropicissimo plantings.

I answered a call one day from Long Island, New York. It was Dennis Schrader, a renowned nurseryman specializing in tropicals. He had run across my name in Florida and wanted to come for a visit. This was a giant stroke to my ego because Dennis's book, Hot Plants for Cool Places, was hugely popular.

He arrived one stifling late-summer morning, having driven from Long Island in a truck so he could take plenty of plants back with him. We immediately took a walk through the Garden.

"You know this is totally new," he pointed out. "Unlike the Victorian tropical trend, you aren't doing the trick of making traditional gardens with tropical plants. You're going full-in, making jungle-like environs."

Dennis took photos as we walked. We took cuttings and pulled things up for him to take back.

He asked if we could visit the Garden again at dusk, and then launched into more conversation, "We're trying this approach in New York."

"Nancy Goodwin and Edith Eddleman are doing it in North Carolina, too," he expanded. "But you have a totally different climate from all of us. You put these plants out, and they explode. The fast growth coupled with the immersive scale of it makes for some really cutting-edge design."

As he spoke, I looked around to see the Garden through his eyes.

"It is…," Dennis stopped mid-sentence searching for the right word. "It is transportive, Jenks. Mind blowing."

I forgot to include Melodie on this tour.

At home later, with a baby in her arms, Melodie quietly confided in me, "I have been doing the groundwork of planting and testing tropicals for years."

She gently shifts her baby and continues, "But it was all in hidden places throughout the Zoo. Then you and Jim ran with it and planted tropicals on a big scale in the Garden. Now, everyone oohs and aahs at those plantings."

"Oh, Mel, I'm so sorry," I said as my heart sank. "I should have called you to meet Dennis this morning. You know I can't do this without you. I couldn't even have gotten through Clemson without you."

That wasn't entirely true, but it was close.

I brought up an old memory from college, "Remember? You were the first woman in Clemson Ag Forestry Club. When the Good Ole Boys tried to thwart you with a tobacco chewing contest. You won it."

'I don't want to be like Jim," I added, "always hogging the spotlight."

She cracked a smile. Whenever Melodie and I needed a scapegoat, Jim was it. We loved him, but he was just too easy of a target.

Melodie's personal tropicissimo plant list not only informed the Garden, but local nurseries, too. Between our orders and those of one pioneering nursery who jumped on the bandwagon, we convinced San Felasco, a major Florida nursery, to deliver weekly to Columbia. This led to city streets and suburban houses taking on the tropicissimo look.

Everything we gardeners did depended on working hand in hand with other groups — not only the ones from the big black-tie party who had money but also landscapers, nurseries, city horticulturists, trucking companies, writers, and newspaper journalists. With everyone onboard, the trend spread through towns all over the state.

Anticipating huge plants by the end of summer, we built massive supports for them and sturdy trellises to host vines. We used giant bamboo from the Zoo to make crazy, soaring supports that looked like two matching 18-foot teepees interwoven with thick supple wisteria vines. Then an arch of bamboo, reinforced with PVC, stretched over a sidewalk between the two bamboo and wisteria teepees. They supported top-heavy, 15-foot candelabra flowers and Zanzibar castor beans. The bamboo arch held silver stems of wooly morning glory vines, tying the Garden beds together.

By mid-summer the vines and structures gave us a surprise. The bamboo arches came to life thanks to the silver felt of the morning glory vines collecting evening dew. Each morning the structures dipped under the added weight. Then, with the heat of the day, they would slowly shift back into the form of a proper arch.

Those arch displays caught the attention of HGTV, and the network sent photographers to the Garden to document them for The 25 Best Gardens in the United States, a guidebook that helped to put Riverbanks on the map as a botanical destination.

The popular magazine Southern Living sent their folks, too.

One evening as the sun set, a former Zoo horticulture intern who had become a Southern Living writer, directed Melodie and me to the ideal spot for the perfect photo. She was writing an article about the plants but was leading with the people who loved them. She directed us to step into waist-deep foliage, then to prop ourselves against a low wall made of curvy balustrades.

I loved this moment in the setting sun. We rested against Jim's favorite English-style wall and leaned into each other while plants from Melodie's tropicissimo plants swirled around us.

❧

27: Magnolia Years

Today, 30 years after we built the Garden, the plantings have filled out. Trees now cast shade, and shrubs overflow their spaces. Plants and people and dreams have matured and died.

Back then — which seems like magnolia years ago — personalities and conflicts grew. We idealize growth as a positive word, but growth tears things apart, too. We misfits planted a garden, cultivated creativity, and changed the garden styles of our town. Like all things that grow, some stay strong, some rot, and some die young. Magnolia trees, prehistoric beings that live for centuries, resist rot.

If you and I toured the Garden today, we'd see different layers, different dimensions, even different stories. At a particular spot in the summer shrub border, I'd point out an empty space. That's where one of Dr. J.C. Raulston's plant gifts, a tree called 'Jade Snowflake', lived. Rare and beloved back then, it dropped seeds that sprang up like cancer trying to take over the bed. For a while we chopped it back every winter, preventing flowers and seeds.

That tree is long gone now. Maybe years of cutting it back shortened its life, or maybe a new gardener correctly thought that a botanical garden shouldn't glorify such an environmental pest of a plant. 'Jade Snowflake' could have lived decades longer than I ever will, but its life was cut short.

J.C.'s life was cut short too. One tired night on a road near Asheboro, North Carolina, J.C. took his place with the Uncles. But I still feel him put his arm around me sometimes and hear him say, "Don't worry about that bothersome critic. Go out in the garden. Plants won't hurt you."

As you and I continued to walk past the gate in the wall across from the little brick gazebo, we'd see the brick walkways, the walls, the wrought iron, and all the structures that are the same as they ever were. But most of the plants have aged out. Some died. One huge clump of crinum needs dividing. Deep in the clump, one bulb has grown too much. It's a garden after all.

"Hold on a minute," I'd tell you as I stepped around the wall. "Wait here. After my prostate started its old man growth spurt two years ago…" my explanation would trail off as I shrug, turn away, and unzip.

After I rejoined you, I'd guide us to a gate with a clematis growing through it. In my mind I'd recall my Daddy walking by that same gate years ago with a panicked expression on his face. He had looked at me helplessly and started jogging off toward the men's room.

His generation of gentlemen was too proud to do what I'd just done in front of you. Following my father into the men's room 15 minutes later, I found him trying to dry his pants under the hand dryer. Here was my strong, capable old man, embarrassed, not able to control his body.

When Daddy died, he was only 74 — just 30 in magnolia years. I wish that before cancer got him, we would have talked. He could have told me, tried to help me understand, or helped prepare me for how my body would change.

When Daddy and I left the men's room those years ago, we found Momma gazing out over the Garden through the canopy of seven-sons trees. Back when the Garden was new, I'd planted those rare, expensive trees and dreamed they'd last forever. In a cooler climate, they could have, but in our heat, in our soil, a fungus grew into the roots.

Did Momma see the beauty or the inevitable decline? Both?

If you continued with me on our stroll, we'd encounter the purple-leaf azalea that a new young gardener recently planted along with a golden coleus called 'Jimmy's Sunshine.' Melodie, who still manages this Garden, had named the plant for her husband — one-eared Jimmy. It reminded her of her beefy, country Jimmy who, on our staff field trip so many years ago, rode up the elevator in the Atlanta hotel holding on to his wife's luggage and dresses.

I can hear his throaty laugh now as he asks, "Jenks, do you think those gay rodeo cowboys in the elevator thought these were my dresses?"

A great stay-at-home daddy and an indulgent husband, Jimmy was my friend and the best splinter remover in the world. He hosted Riverbanks's volunteer parties, loaded plants, and waited in too many hot cars while Melodie and I shopped for seeds. One particularly cruel summer, he took a day for himself to play golf. Melodie and her two little children came home to find Jimmy on the couch with his heart stopped. He was only 40.

In May I plant veggies, and on a hot July afternoon I pick a basket of fresh eggplants. I'll fry them up for supper and head to bed. The next morning, when I get up, I see that the entire plant is drooping. A vole, rat, or some other little bastard has gnawed it right off, leaving a sharp, definite, final cut. It seems sudden, but that rat has been gnawing for days just below the surface, trying to get to the arteries that connect life-supporting roots to the parts we all see, love, and eat.

These moments remind me of Jimmy and the unfairness of eggplant years.

Heading out of the Walled Garden, you and I would go through the Antique Rose Garden. It struggles with rose rosette virus now. It'll probably get plowed up soon. But 20 years ago, when the roses were in their prime, they were a testament to the seminal breeding that happened near here.

I'd probably point out the stone arch in the corner of the Antique Rose Garden. Some might like to pretend that the arch and its location were meticulously planned, but it's not true. The arch is where it is because one day Jim Martin said to me, "We're getting access to some spectacular granite blocks. Build a stone arch. Maybe here."

I see Jim in every crevice of this garden. Over the years he's moved on to spread his enduring vision of creative, accessible gardening to the most important gardens across the state.

If you and I walked beyond the arch, our feet would hit a narrow asphalt path. Back then, our crew used wheelbarrows to move two tons of asphalt miles down the slope. By building this path with shovels instead of tractors, we were able to save venerable old trees.

One hundred and sixty years before our work on this slope, prison laborers cut blocks from these granite cliffs. The blocks were used to build the South Carolina Department of Corrections penitentiary, one of the oldest prisons in the country. My friend Eric, who worked there just before it closed, arranged a tour of the locked-down cell blocks for us.

That penitentiary was the mustiest, heaviest, most infused-with-sadness building I had ever been in. Eric and I were allowed to tag some of the massive stones so they could be brought back to the Garden after the penitentiary had been demolished.

Choosing blocks of granite for the Garden, I couldn't help but notice the layers of graffiti that the inmates had added. It made me wonder if out in some nursing home or on a street corner, some of the inmates, perhaps a Daisy Dukes gender-bending baseball player, survived to tell the stories behind all that graffiti.

In the heat of summer when I came back to work on Saturday afternoons to water the pots, Eric would meet me and help. After watering, he and I would walk through the stone arch, and along this narrow asphalt path, then veer off to follow an old swimmer trail to an ancient stone-walled canal. Its black water was as smooth as a slide. There was a constant murmur there, the noise of water moving and the sound of the breeze it created.

In that total isolation of this almost sacred place, Eric and I would strip, leap, and swim in the cold black water.

We would wade over to a little island of granite boulders in the middle of the river. A few green ash trees shaded dwarf palmettos at the water's edge.

The palmettos' leaves came up all twisted from softball-sized lumps, skewed by growing around rock down in the muck. During one of our visits to that island, we dug our hands into the fragrant muck, feeling for the lump, trying to pull one up to take it home. The sludge coated our forearms and foreheads. Then we anointed each other with sacred black mud. After washing the mud off our bodies in the brown, bracing water, we felt so strong and so connected to our forest.

If you and I walked along the asphalt path, my mind would wander to memories of Eric as we pass a white oak, whose seedlings come up with tiny half-white leaves. These enchanting, new leaves are thin as a tissue and spread out to try to catch light, to make energy, to grow. But they can't. The genes that make them a beautiful white color also weaken them. They die young. The tree's beauty is a fatal flaw. We had tried digging them up, and then carefully potting them. Yet those beautiful weaklings still died and all too quickly.

Some hidden thing deep in Eric's beautiful skull was his fatal flaw. I would wheel his chair onto his screen porch and light a cigarette for him. We would sit and listen to the river murmur. By then Eric spoke in something like a toddler's language.

One night we were sitting on his porch and looking over the river. We remembered those twisted palms, stripping down, mud all over us, and the high of jumping in that frigid water.

For a few minutes, he was the clear, well-spoken Eric. Then he said "Let's jump in the whiskey."

When I walk those river banks, I see a flow of inviting dark liquor, creamy white oak seedlings, and I hear Eric, born beautiful and gone too soon.

His lover Bob lives with me now in the house that Pat and I had made a home for so many people. Pat ended up in a city far away with a happy home, his own family, and a dog. They all visit sometimes. In those special moments, we reminisce and laugh, but always feel the swelling in our hearts and throats.

I don't know why I seem to have gotten magnolia years, while some really good people got eggplant years or white oak years. It's one of those things I think about whenever I'm in the Garden.

———

I know a magnolia tree where someone carved a love heart with initials decades ago. Most of this declaration of love endures — the heart and two of the letters (H.E.). The remaining letters have become illegible, just a scar in the bark. I want to write a story about young H.E., declaring his love on this tree. He set out to make this declaration with intention. He brought the pocket knife. He searched for the perfect spot. He carved for hours. Alone. Dreaming. He or maybe she. Black or maybe White. Straight or maybe not. Our stories live on for magnolia years.

Epilogue: Gardening in Black and White

I said from the outset that I wanted to plant gardens magical and beautiful enough to attract all kinds of people. Today if you go to Riverbanks Botanical Garden on a busy Saturday, you'll notice that the crowd is mostly White people and Latino people. In South Carolina Black people make up 26 percent of the population but are noticeably absent in public gardens. Our Garden is not an exception to that deficit in diversity.

People ask me today what I would have done differently in making the Riverbanks Botanical Garden. I know the answer right away. It's scattered through these stories, and something I had considered but never acted on. I would have taken into greater consideration that centuries of racism excluded Black people. We all suffer because of it, and our Southern gardens lack untold beauty, layers, and plant diversity because of racial divides. I would have tried harder to include elements of Black culture, heritage, gardening history, and unique experience with plants.

———

When the Garden was brand new, visitors gazed over a ribbon of water cascading to the gazebo. Flanking each side, diamond-shaped beds, brick paths, and limestone-capped walls. The original plan included formal boxwood hedges outlining each bed. The vision was based on formal, geometric gardens of the past. We, the garden disruptors, wholeheartedly rejected that formality and its accompanying baggage.

To me, it was a view of domination over nature. Formal gardens are often designed and meant to be enjoyed from above. The experience of being in Southern formal gardens is often unpleasant, broiling, hot, and bland. I see those gardens and think of the poor sods who spend brutal hours pruning in the hot sun to achieve lollipop and square shapes that seldom occur in Nature.

I know that in the South, those Antebellum gardens were possible only with enslaved labor. That's not speculation. I've worked in formal gardens with hedges, parterres, and topiaries. I've worked with the crews, counted the man hours, and purchased the equipment and chemicals needed to keep a hedge.

In our growth-producing climate, pruning has to be done every six weeks between March and September. There is winter rejuvenation and depth pruning. Today's complex hedge gardens are possible only with chemical growth retardants; noisy, air-polluting power equipment; and, too often, underpaid labor.

We nixed the plans for hedges in the original Garden plans but couldn't change the existing geometric walkways. So we let plants soften them. The swamp lilies that Porter and I collected early on from an abandoned building near the Branchville barber shop flanked the canal. Those lilies did something much more important. They came to represent the racial divide that plagues Southern souls and society.

Initially we thought these plants, collected along the Edisto River, were native, *Crinum americanum*. On closer inspection we identified them as a similar species introduced from the Caribbean. Like lots of South Carolina history, food, and architecture, they may have come from Barbados or Trinidad.

As Colonial planters overplanted and overpopulated those islands, their siblings and sons sought the greener pastures of undeveloped coastal South Carolina. We know their stories, and we know the plants they brought with them that built fortunes — indigo, cotton, and rice. We know these immigrant planters designed formal pleasure gardens lined with green boxwood hedges, meant to be seen from the veranda.

We don't know as much about the enslaved people who actually did the farming and gardening nor the plants they brought for food, flowers, and pharmacy. Could this Caribbean crinum, long naturalized in the local swamps, be part of that unwritten history?

The hidden history of how African plants and gardening techniques influence the South is slowly being revealed today. The history of rice technology is a perfect example of how long a hidden history can take to be uncovered. As recently as the 1970s, very few people recognized that Africans had brought the floodgates and cultivation methods that powered Southern rice production for a century and established eating preferences that endure today.

In his 1974 seminal book, Black Majority, historian Peter Wood brought attention to African rice systems perpetuated in the U.S. by slaves from the Rice Coast of West Africa. As recently as the 1990s, Dr. Judith Carney, author of Black Rice: The African Origins of Rice Cultivation in the Americas, examined the environments, technologies, and methods of rice cultivation across the Atlantic to show the connection between cultivation in Africa and America. It's taken decades to become common knowledge.

In a conversation about flowers, including crinum, Dr. Carney told me:

> Many African plants served as medicines and foods on slave ships. Some of these plants were listed as ship's provisions or medicines. Others came on board by chance as seeds in necklaces or as undocumented acquisitions in African ports of departure. These plants usually aren't mentioned because they were part of the routine business of provisioning ships to deliver human "merchandise" to slave ports of the Americas. With the threat of a

slave uprising constant and lethal fevers present, ship captains only casually mentioned, if at all, the provisions they purchased in Africa. This accounts for the silence as well as the pedestrian nature of what they stocked to effect an Atlantic crossing. However, any provisions remaining from a slave voyage would have little purpose to ship captains once they disembarked their enslaved passengers at the auction blocks of slave societies. But these plant materials, be they seeds, tubers, beans, or bulbs would certainly have had value and meaning to those brought from Africa to new lands and terrifying circumstances.

A plant with medicinal use could easily have traveled here among enslaved people. They practiced medicine widely and often knew cures that were valued by White enslavers. The Colonial Assembly that governed South Carolina in the 1700s freed two enslaved men, Caesar and Sampson, for sharing their vast knowledge of botanical medicines, including antidotes to rattlesnake venom and other poisons.

African medicine people traveled frequently from plantation to plantation, but their knowledge could be used to make poison, too. This possibility threatened and frightened White people, particularly in the South, where so many enslaved herbalists and medical practitioners were living. That fear, front and center among the White population, led to the South Carolina General Assembly's passing a law in 1749 that prohibited enslaved people from "being employed by physicians to concoct poisons or administer medicine of any kind."

The medicinal properties of crinum are well-documented around the world, especially in western Africa, the original home of many of the people who were enslaved by Europeans. Crinum planted on graves there were believed to protect the dead on their afterlife journey. Marquetta Goodwine, founder of the Gullah/Geechee Sea Island Coalition and elected Queen of the Gullah Nation, told me, "That also means crinum connect us to the world of the ancestors."

These cultural and medicinal uses were powerful connections that drove people to find a way to carry crinum along on even arduous journeys. Those connections could be part of why crinum got the reputation as Black people's plants.

Could our swamp bells — the Caribbean crinum plants now growing along the canal gardens at Riverbanks — have been incorporated into the "rootwork," medicine, or religion of enslaved Africans in the Caribbean waiting to be trafficked to other parts of the world? Could the slaves have somehow managed to hide some of these plants to take with them when they were shipped to Carolina?

The plant we call swamp bells certainly looks like the kind of plant that these displaced Africans already knew from home. It smells like it, grows like it, and it could have become a substitute for the similar species used in Africa. Can we authenticate this with written documents? Probably not.

While researchers investigate these topics today, back in 1991 we had fewer resources to consult. I asked but got no answers. Most of the people I would like to have asked died years ago. The few remaining who might have held those passed-down secrets didn't talk. Why would they have talked about their ancestors' knowledge to a young White man from the Zoo?

———

The racial divisions that sparked terms like "Black people's plants" may seem antiquated today, but they persist in society and are evidenced in the speech and actions of individuals. I believe it's important to write down instances that exemplify racial divisions, to talk about them, and to commit them to history.

My friend Babs Bruns helped me understand how racial division, including the racial associations of certain plants, grew over time. She grew up in the 1940s on her family's sprawling farm. It wasn't a plantation. Just a big peach farm. As a White girl, living far out in the country, she grew up playing with workers' children, Black and White, but she also learned the rules of race. She could play outside with certain children. She could go on the porch. She couldn't go into certain folks' houses or invite certain children into hers.

Babs loved flowers, so she learned who had which plants. She waxed poetic, describing a friend's home, the front porch of a Black tenant farmer's shack.

"Miss Myrtus had flowers in pots on the porch," she recounted to me. "She had a lot of crinum lilies in the side yard, and cannas, and catalpa trees."

I interrupted her. "How about in your mother's garden? Did your Mother have any of those? How about crinum?"

She was adamant. "Nope. Most definitely not. Those were all Black people's plants. You simply couldn't have had them or any of those things back then. In fact, the rule in Mother's garden was no flowers in the front yard. No vegetables. At all. No pickup trucks or farm machinery could ever be in the front yard. Only green plants, boxwood hedges, and maybe a white camellia."

Even today lots of folks know and understand the unofficial list of plants associated with race. The stigmas have diminished rapidly but are not entirely gone. Babs and I wondered if those associations were part of Jim Crow-era divisions designed to establish and illustrate all sorts of cultural divisions between Black and White people.

I recalled my family and lots of White people who also had crinum. The rules had exceptions.

I called Felder Rushing, whose 1993 award-winning book, Pass-Along Plants, told the stories of these underappreciated, old plants. Felder knew about the people who grew them and the people who looked at them with contempt. He told me:

> What you're talking about are plants that share easily. That means they can be shared any time of year. You can pull up a bit of that daylily on the hottest day in July, and it'll live. Think about it. That's when poor people have time to get a bit of a plant. These are plants that get shared by people who don't have time or money to plan a trip to the nursery or to buy via mail order. You get a piece of it that may then sit under a bush for a day or two until you can plant it. A month later, it's beautiful, and a year later, you're passing it on to a friend.

Basically it's the same five or ten plants no matter where you go in the world: double orange daylilies, cannas, zinnias, and that old white peony with the red spot, and lilies like crinum.

Felder said of crinum, "These are poor people's plants. As people get off the farm and get more sophisticated, they all seek to create divisions between them and poor people."

The South's slow change led millions, especially Black people, to migrate north and west and into the suburbs.

In the rural Deep South, right up until the 1970s, many poor people lived much as they had at the beginning of the century. My mother rode on a mule-drawn cart in the 1950s. Her friend had a mule to plow his garden until 1970. They grew the same flowers, herbs, and vegetables that you'd have seen in 1920.

As Felder suggested, what I knew as Black people plants could just as easily be called White trash plants, po' buckra' plants, Sandlapper plants, or Georgia cracker plants. Around the world, they have similar baggage: wetback plants, Thai trailer trash, or insert-your-own-slur-here plants.

Felder helped me understand that categories like this let people put themselves above other people. We do it with clothes, cars, styles, and even professions, especially in agricultural professions like horticulture. It's not unique to the South or only about race. However, we were in the South, where this was most often about race.

———

Melodie, Jim, and I reached out from the start and brought in people not usually a part of botanical garden planning. Staff and volunteers came from all walks of life. We realized that over a quarter of our state's population was underrepresented on our staff. I met so many Black people who had, and still have, a generations-long love for the cultivation of the land.

We recognized we had a gap. We recognized the loss due to that gap. For example, if we'd had some young Black staff, they might have helped with the crinum question. They might have said, "Hey, I'll ask my grandma. She grows that plant. I think she uses the roots for something."

———

My own prejudice came into play. I'd been asked early on to go to the labor pick-up point for the Garden's workforce. At the time, before the influx of Latin Americans, the guys at the labor stand were all Black. I solidly refused. My objection was not based on race but on experience working with day laborers who had no commitment to a project and would work a few days, uninspired, then move on without notice. That choice could have made me miss meeting any men who knew about Black people's plants.

I'd missed other opportunities too. Remember Rosey, the yard man who'd brought camellias to us early on? He was the man who was referred to by his camellia-growing boss, as "my man Rosey." I could have asked him, or I could have asked as a guest at the Wisteria Garden Club, one of the only remaining Black garden clubs in the United States. Anytime I spoke to a White Garden Club, at least one person would pass me the phone number of a son, daughter, or friend who "would love to come work and learn." That didn't happen with the ladies of the Black clubs. I should have asked clearly and frequently.

Another example of a missed opportunity because I didn't know how to ask was when the hosts of the "Sista' Talk" radio show invited me to talk about the Garden during an on-air interview. I talked about new flowers, but I should have said, "Y'all, the food, the baskets, the language of your Geechee grandparents, the medicine and religion of your African ancestors are integral parts of my life; but I haven't always recognized that. I don't know how to bring those things into this Garden. Who has a son or daughter or friend who'd like to join us?"

Another part of the answer to the lack of Black professional gardeners isn't hidden. Do you think Rosey's children ever once said to their children, "Why don't you become a gardener? You can be like your grandpa?" If they were to say that, it would be a threat, possibly providing motivation to do better, not a serious career proposal.

Plenty of rural people, including me, had never heard of a career as a horticulturist, garden designer, or landscaper. We knew "yard men." We knew people who got underpaid to cut grass, shear hedges, and rake leaves. That's hardly an inspiration for a career choice.

My office mate Jack, a Michigan farm boy, had said the same thing: "I'd never heard of a botanical garden. I got off a bus one day, as an adult, a soldier in Korea, and wandered around and fell in love with my wife and with bonsai."

Even though I had always loved plants, I never considered them a career until college, when I suddenly saw all sorts of new things, including my first botanical garden. Once there, I understood how to use and navigate the system. I'd been groomed for it. I knew how to talk to the old-school professors. I knew how to call on and get invitations from mentors, as I'd done with then-famous Dr. J.C. Raulston. Lifelong interactions with the Uncles had even given me certain advantages. Most importantly, I had the privilege of having parents who partially paid for college.

I had played in the swamp with a childhood friend who lived through the woods and down a dirt road from me. Same woods, same love of nature, same education, and the same community. Different races. If we had gone to the same college and had the same major, he would have found roadblocks, burdens, and suspicion in the same places where I had found opportunity and had gotten help navigating the formal and informal systems of college.

———

Symmetrical gardens of hedges like you'd see in Antebellum gardens convey a message of human domination over nature. As did the university system. The message I got, even as a boy, from those gardens was "You can work here. You can trim the hedges and sweat and be a yard man." Even though I've made a career of gardening, I still feel it today.

Like formality in gardens, the horticulture career path creates a place where a certain class of White guys can manage and design while other races can only labor.

We did have two Black men among our 16 gardeners and crowd of volunteers. I had hoped they would help out with the crinum questions about race. That hope reveals another racial prejudice — equating Black people in the South as rural and connected to the earth. One of those young gardeners grew up in an Upstate city. He had no remaining connections to rural or Gullah culture. The other Black volunteer was older, a military retiree, born in Japan and educated at Rutgers. He thought talking about the racial component I wanted to explore would deepen divisions.

Both of those gardeners represented people of the Great Migration. That "uplifting" of Black people severed the knowledge chain that might have answered crinum questions. There were, however, the people who had stayed behind. These were mostly coastal Gullah or Geechee people as well as others who'd maintained a more rural lifestyle. For them, agriculture represented poverty. Gardening seemed a lot like agriculture.

Social activist and lover of the land, bell hooks [sic] wrote about the intersectionality of race, capitalism, gender, and oppression.

"Most people imagine that black folks working the land were just victims, working for little and living a starvation life. We...know that the life of a small farmer can be terribly hard. What outsiders rarely see is the spiritual reward — the power of redemptive suffering. When you live in a capitalist culture that tells you all forms of suffering are bad (take this pill, this shot, have this operation, make the pain go away), then you lose the mystery and magic of redemptive suffering."

Most gardeners are like me and choose to engage, even revel, in heat, sweat, sore muscles, and rashes from insect bites or poisonous leaves. It's not always fun but it's always immersive, connecting, and satisfying.

Sometimes, at the Garden, when we squat in the sun to pull weeds, we hear visitors telling their children, "Look, that's why I tell you to study. If you don't study, you may end up pulling weeds like that guy."

While redemptive suffering doesn't pay the bills or contribute to feeling valued, I could choose to afford it.

———

The divide over race, created by my forefathers and perpetuated by my parents and me, hurts our gardens. We lack perspective and connection to Black people even as we work under Zanzibar castor beans, Cape lilies, Orange River lilies, acres of Coleus, and dozens of other plants brought from Africa.

The core principle of ecology is that what matters resides in relationships rather than in things. Garden design often misses this point. The grand view of expansive geometric beds, pergolas, and canals focuses on things and on man's control over things. Those curling border hedges of formal gardens are no longer plants but walls.

There's an ancient divide among garden designers, horticulturists, gardeners, and garden visitors.

There are entire books written to exalt the joys of one style over the other. But there's no doubt that one style represents domination over nature and glorifies the artificial over the natural. The mechanisms of formal gardens are similar to the mechanisms of culture that favor and support certain people while excluding others from careers in horticulture. Sometimes with subtlety, sometimes with concealed enmity, some gardens convey that White men are in charge and that other people are not welcome.

Back in the 1990s, Jim, in a suit and tie, would usher the donors, potential rental customers, and brides to the overlook of the fountain cascade at the Garden. They admired the grand view. We gardeners squatted, weeded, and chatted in the flowers. We were part of their view.

And they were part of ours. I wanted to call them down, into the plants, into the life of the garden. I wanted them to see it from here. I knew they could see it, understand it, feel it, if only they didn't stand apart.

It's easier to feel connected from within a garden, to feel the ecology and the relationship between things, especially for those of us who have experienced gardens mostly as pleasure places. Domination isn't inherent in gardens. It's been built in with intentional, subtle, complex layers. Racism and the disconnection between people, plants, and living things can be healed if we recognize and try to bridge the divide that exists in all parts of our lives. Especially in gardens.

Deep Rooted Wisdom: Skills and Stories From Generations of Gardeners

Jenks uses his natural storytelling abilities to pass on the art and science of gardening. Lessons gleaned from his mentors offer connections to a younger generation. Each chapter focuses on one person and one lesson. More than recounting myths, this book updates country wisdom of soil science, propagation, and organic gardening with recent science and how-to-lessons.

Funky Little Flower Farm

In 24 stories organized by month, Jenks shares plants and skills developed through a gardening life. You'll come to know this 18th-century farm turned pioneering organic nursery, its caretakers, and its plants. Director of the National Arboretum, Dr. Richard Olsen, says, "Jenks writes with a much-needed shot of authenticity. As you take in stories and images from these pages, you'll come to understand, in a poignant way, how to become a gardener in the Deep South.

Crinum; Unearthing The History Of The World's Biggest Bulb

In the only book ever written devoted to the genus Crinum, delve into stories of its medicinal use, history, and geography. Lovely color photos, charts, and personal experiences collected by crinum lovers from across the United States show readers how to use the giant bulbs in their own gardens.

Jenks also writes weekly essays in a series called PlantPeoples on Substack.com

www.ingramcontent.com/pod-product-compliance
Lightning Source LLC
Chambersburg PA
CBHW022135080426
42734CB00006B/365